Simply Gorgeous.

iPhone: The Missing Manual
By David Pogue
ISBN 0596513747
$19.99 US / 23.99 CAN

No surprise, the iPhone is gorgeous. *iPhone: The Missing Manual* is a book as breathtaking as its subject. Teeming with high-quality color graphics, each custom designed page helps you accomplish specific tasks—everything from Web browsing to watching videos. Written by *New York Times* columnist and *Missing Manual* series creator David Pogue, this book shows you how to get the most out of your new Apple iPhone.

Find the new *iPhone: The Missing Manual* and other *Missing Manuals*
at your favorite bookseller, or online at www.missingmanuals.com

THE MISSING MANUALS
The books that should have been in the box

POGUE PRESS™
O'REILLY®

Craft:

Volume 06

transforming traditional crafts™

Special Section PLAY

Columns

Features

Vol. 06, Feb. 2008. CRAFT (ISSN 1932-9121) is published 4 times a year by O'Reilly Media, Inc. in the months of January, April, July, and October. O'Reilly Media is located at 1005 Gravenstein Hwy. North, Sebastopol, CA 95472, (707) 827-7000. SUBSCRIPTIONS: Send all subscription requests to CRAFT, P.O. Box 17046, North Hollywood, CA 91615-9588 or subscribe online at craftzine.com/subscribe or via phone at (866) 368-5652 (U.S. and Canada), all other countries call (818) 487-2037. Subscriptions are available for $34.95 for 1 year (4 issues) in the United States; in Canada: $39.95 USD; all other countries: $49.95 USD. Application to Mail at Periodicals Postage Rates is Pending at Sebastopol, CA, and at additional mailing offices. POSTMASTER: Send address changes to CRAFT, P.O. Box 17046, North Hollywood, CA 91615-9588. Canada Post Publications Mail Agreement Number 41129568. Canada Postmaster: Send address changes to: O'Reilly Media, PO Box 456, Niagara Falls, ON L2E 6V2.

Carla Sinclair
Welcome

>> Carla Sinclair is editor-in-chief of CRAFT magazine.
carla@craftzine.com

Go With Your Flow

Flow is the mental state of operation in which the person is fully immersed in what he or she is doing, characterized by a feeling of energized focus, full involvement, and success in the process of the activity.

—*Wikipedia*

When we first decided to devote this volume to Play, I mentioned to the other CRAFT editors that, in a way, you're playing when you craft. I wasn't sure if they got what I meant, since I myself wasn't quite sure *why* I thought playing and crafting were intertwined. Later, as I tried to define my thoughts, I realized that it wasn't the activities that were related as much as the experience of getting lost in the moment that both crafting and playing sometimes produced.

We've all experienced it, that Zen-like ecstasy of becoming one with what you're doing when fully engaged in an activity. All other thoughts and worries, as well as a sense of time, vanish during this elevated state. Athletes call it "in the zone," jazz musicians have called it "in the groove," but I like referring to it as "flow," a term coined by psychologist Mihaly Csikszentmihalyi, author of *Finding Flow* (Basic Books).

Csikszentmihalyi explains that a flow state happens when we become so focused on an activity that, similar to a deep state of meditation, we block out all other distractions and become completely immersed in the task at hand. Hours seem to pass both instantaneously and indefinitely, and afterward we're left with a deep sense of well-being.

I've tripped on flow from all kinds of activities, losing myself while acting in a school play, weeding the garden around my porch, practicing the piano, competing in a tennis tournament, embroidering a tea towel, even painting a rock to make a paperweight. In all these instances the concept of time disappeared, and my mind — feeling strangely electric and calm simultaneously — became one with the activity.

Although flow isn't partial to crafting and playing — I have turned on the flow while reading a book, editing an article, and driving long distances, for example — Csikszentmihalyi rates the "active leisures" of crafting and playing as activities that most frequently produce a flow state. The trick to finding flow is to choose a project — or game or hobby — that is challenging enough to capture your complete interest without being so difficult that you want to prematurely throw in the towel.

We've all experienced it, that Zen-like ecstasy of becoming one with what you're doing.

Anyone hoping to get their flow on will have countless opportunities with the dozens of projects in these pages. You might find your flow while making, or later playing with, the flashing LED hula hoop (*page 54*), adorable Japanese "otedama" juggling toys (*page 50*), personalized coloring book (*page 48*), or thumb piano made from objects found around the house (*page 38*).

But of course crafting itself offers flow whether it's playful or not, and so we also offer the usual eclectic mix of projects (sew a T-shirt wedding dress, stitch plushie monsters, build a kerosene lantern chandelier, make solar-lit jewelry, and much more) that will appeal to crafters of all skill levels.

"It is the full involvement of flow, rather than happiness, that makes for excellence in life," says Csikszentmihalyi. So let the games — and the crafting — flow! ✄

Craft:™ Projects

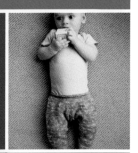

R egarding the origami "Three Dollar Flower" (see CRAFT, Volume 05, page 52): Everything made sense (sort of) up to Step 18 ... and then, voilà, we make a quantum leap to Step 19 with virtually no explanation other than "fold it back up." Huh? I'm supposed to fold up 3 pieces of paper that are all offset at odd angles, but they should look exactly like the 1 piece of paper as it appears in Step 15?

Please consider testing your instructions on a real person before you publish them. No, I'm really not as cranky as I sound ... but c'mon, if you're gonna show us a really cool way to leave a three-dollar tip, please give us the real deal, OK? —Jim Kofalt

Thanks for writing, Jim. We test our projects, big or little, and this one was no exception. Our interns agreed that step was tricky, but doable, as they showed us the final product before we printed the magazine. But we know that origami steps can be hard to illustrate in limited space, so after reading your note, we've produced a video podcast of the Three Dollar Flower (pictured above), plus an expanded PDF illustration, at makezine.com/go/ flowerpodcast. Here's hoping they help you easily fold the flower!

I 'm an avid reader of CRAFT and a huge admirer of the indie craft world in general. I'm continually inspired by blogs, Flickr groups, Etsy, etc. I love the DIY spirit, the sense of community, and the freedom to bend (or break!) the rules.

But I'm often puzzled by the dismissive and condescending attitude in the craft world toward scrapbooking (see CRAFT, Volume 05, page 12, "Crafting Is for Lovers" by Jean Railla). As a crafter and a scrapbooker, I don't get this. Crafts like crochet and knitting, which used to be the domain of little old ladies, are OK, but scrapbooking is not?

I recognize that scrapbooking is often viewed as the world of teddy bear stickers and soccer moms, but that simply isn't the case anymore. Look at the artistic and inventive work of scrapbookers like Emily Falconbridge, Ali Edwards, or Cathy Zielske. These are women recording their own histories in creative and beautiful ways — telling their own stories, not just highlighting photos of their children's dance recitals.

Having said that, what if all scrapbookers were suburban moms arranging photographs of their children? Would that make it OK to dismiss this form of craft, just because it didn't conform to some kind of hipster definition of what was "cool craft" and what wasn't? —Callie Appelstein

Thank you for your letter, Callie. Most (if not all) of us at CRAFT agree with you — we've run scrapbooking projects in the last few issues and plan to run more.

Like all our columnists, Jean Railla shares her opinions; similar to the op-ed page of a newspaper, our columnists have their own points of view that we hope our readers enjoy, even if they don't always agree.

Also, I think Jean was confessing to the very bias you're speaking of, and taking herself (and other crafters) to task for this bias, in acknowledging that iMovie is basically digital scrapbooking.

I'm sorry you didn't enjoy this particular column, but I hope you continue to enjoy CRAFT as a whole.

—Carla Sinclair

 Got something to say? Write to us at editor@craftzine.com.

Craft:™ Volume 06

Crafter Profiles

26

DIY

Make Cool Stuff

ON THE COVER

These mix-and-match monster plushies were made by Moxie, who believes that every creature should be unique. She shows you how to make your own original beast on page 60. Photographed by Garry McLeod and styled by Alex Murphy. Chair illustration by Alison Kendall.

Craft:
transforming traditional crafts™

EDITOR AND PUBLISHER
Dale Dougherty
dale@oreilly.com

EDITOR-IN-CHIEF
Carla Sinclair
carla@craftzine.com

CREATIVE DIRECTOR
Daniel Carter
dcarter@oreilly.com

MANAGING EDITOR
Shawn Connally
shawn@craftzine.com

DESIGNERS
Katie Wilson
Alison Kendall

ASSOCIATE MANAGING EDITOR
Goli Mohammadi
goli@craftzine.com

PRODUCTION DESIGNER
Gerry Arrington

SENIOR EDITOR
Natalie Zee Drieu
nat@craftzine.com

PHOTO EDITOR
Sam Murphy
smurphy@oreilly.com

COPY CHIEF
Keith Hammond

ASSOCIATE PUBLISHER
Dan Woods
dan@oreilly.com

ONLINE MANAGER
Terrie Miller

CIRCULATION DIRECTOR
Heather Harmon

STAFF EDITOR
Arwen O'Reilly

ACCOUNT MANAGER
Katie Dougherty
katie@oreilly.com

CONTRIBUTING EDITOR
Phillip Torrone

MARKETING & EVENTS COORDINATOR
Rob Bullington

CRAFT TECHNICAL ADVISORY BOARD
**Jill Bliss, Jenny Hart, Garth Johnson,
Leah Kramer, Alison Lewis, Matt Maranian,
Ulla-Maaria Mutanen, Kathreen Ricketson**

PUBLISHED BY O'REILLY MEDIA, INC.
Tim O'Reilly, CEO
Laura Baldwin, COO

Visit us online at craftzine.com
Comments may be sent to editor@craftzine.com

For advertising inquiries, contact:
Katie Dougherty, 707-827-7272, katie@oreilly.com

For sponsorship inquiries, contact:
Scott Feen, 707-827-7105, scottf@oreilly.com

For event inquiries, contact:
Sherry Huss, 707-827-7074, sherry@oreilly.com

Contributing Artists:
Melinda Beck, Nick Dragotta, Gabriela Hasbun, Tim Lillis, Phil Marden, Garry McLeod, Jen Siska, Robyn Twomey

Contributing Writers:
Brian Anderson, Susan Beal, sarah-marie belcastro, Alastair Bland, Joost Bonsen, Susie Bright, Annie Buckley, Cathy Callahan, RP Collier, Leah Culver, Andrea DeHart, Anna Dilemna, Nick Dragotta, Diana Eng, Diane Gilleland, Saul Griffith, Anna Hrachovec, Garth Johnson, Mary Beth Klatt, Donna Kroiz, Lauren Kroiz, Summer Block Kumar, Katie Kurtz, Hatti Lim, Stephanie Mallard, Matt Maranian, Erin McKean, Lee Meredith, Brookelynn Morris, Jenny Mountjoy, Moxie, Ulla-Maaria Mutanen, Dolin O'Shea, Bre Pettis, Alice Planas, Jenny Ryan, Wendy Seltzer, Peter Sheridan, Eric Smillie, Wendy Tremayne, Cy Tymony, Megan Mansell Williams, Edwin Wise, Theo Wright, Carolyn Yackel

Interns: Matthew Dalton (engr.), Adrienne Foreman (web), Kris Magri (engr.), Lindsey North (crafts)

NOW GREENER THAN EVER!
CRAFT is now printed on recycled, acid-free paper with 30% post-consumer waste. Subscriber copies of CRAFT, Volume 06, were shipped in recyclable plastic bags.

PLEASE NOTE: Technology, the laws, and limitations imposed by manufacturers and content owners are constantly changing. Thus, some of the projects described may not work, may be inconsistent with current laws or user agreements, or may damage or adversely affect some equipment.
Your safety is your own responsibility, including proper use of equipment and safety gear, and determining whether you have adequate skill and experience. Power tools, electricity, and other resources used for these projects are dangerous, unless used properly and with adequate precautions, including safety gear. Some illustrative photos do not depict safety precautions or equipment, in order to show the project steps more clearly. These projects are not intended for use by children.
Use of the instructions and suggestions in CRAFT is at your own risk. O'Reilly Media, Inc., disclaims all responsibility for any resulting damage, injury, or expense. It is your responsibility to make sure that your activities comply with applicable laws, including copyright.

Customer Service cs@readerservices.craftzine.com
Manage your account online, including change of address at:
craftzine.com/account
866-368-5652 toll-free in U.S. and Canada
818-487-2037, 5 a.m.–5 p.m., Pacific

Diane Gilleland (*Otedama*) lives a pretty darn crafty life in Portland, Ore., which is every bit as cool a town as you've heard it is. When she's not organizing Church of Craft meetings or producing her craft podcast (craftypod.com), she's busy bending the rules of physics in order to make mountains of yarn, beads, fabric, and paper fit into her tiny craft space. She'd give anything for one of those carpetbags Mary Poppins has.

Loud, Hispanic, and funny, **Gabriela Hasbun** (*Raven Hanna photography*) is a freelance photographer born and raised in El Salvador. She currently lives in San Francisco with her husband-to-be, Nick, and their cat, Emma. Gabriela has a deep appreciation for scuba diving, watching *Six Feet Under*, playing tennis, and eating almost any flavor of ice cream (Ciao Bella's coconut gelato is the current favorite). She recently shot a fat-positive story on women in the Bay Area. Check it out on her website, gabrielahasbun.com.

Stephanie Mallard (*Duck Tape iPod Case*) is a beginning engineering artist who makes creative things with convenient materials. She lives in Texas with her mom, dad, cat, and dog. Stephanie likes to invent new crafts in her spare time and look for science projects on the web to do for fun. She particularly loves to put her own spin on old projects. And, of course, she loves duck tape for its fix-all reputation and great crafting possibilities.

A true craftoholic, there's not a craft that **Andrea DeHart** (*Wrap Skirt Project*) hasn't tried at least once. Her mother taught her how to sew at a very young age, and Andrea remembers asking for Barbies, not to play with, but as models for her clothing designs. She lives in San Francisco with her husband, 9-month-old daughter, and two cats. Andrea is also the co-founder of Hell's Belles, a classic car club for women, and cruises around in her '62 Mercury Comet named Roxie. Now that's one Crafty Bitch! craftybitch.com

Saul Griffith (*Howtoons*) has been taking things apart to see how they work since he was a little boy in Australia. He now enjoys putting things together, and is currently working on problems in the field of alternative energy. He recently received a MacArthur "genius" award, although he prefers the term "smarty-pants grant." All his pants have cargo pockets with holes and he hates wearing shoes. His *Howtoons* cohort **Nick Dragotta** eats pens and ink for breakfast and occasionally draws for Marvel Comics. Tucker and Celine are his newest superheroes. howtoons.com

Born and raised on the North Shore of Chicago, **Phil Marden** (*Susie's Home Ec* illustration) spent more than 20 years building his career as an illustrator in New York City. His illustrations have appeared in dozens of newspapers and magazines including *Forbes*, *Fortune*, *Newsweek*, and *The New York Times*. His work has also been animated for TV and films and was featured in the recent remake of *The Stepford Wives*. Having relocated to Portland, Ore., Phil now spends more time writing, printmaking, walking his dog, Ivy, and enjoying frequent lattes. He misses New York pizza. philmarden.com

Wendy Seltzer (*Craft and Copyright*) is a law professor at Northwestern and Harvard who researches intellectual property, privacy, and free expression online. She founded the Chilling Effects Clearinghouse, helping people understand their rights in response to online cease-and-desist threats. Cambridge winters haven't yet turned her into an icicle, and neither have the chilling effects of legal threats online. She occasionally takes a break from legal code to program, and her favorite tool is her home-built MythTV. wendy.seltzer.org

Susie Bright
Susie's Home Ec

» Susie Bright is an amateur dressmaker and a professional writer. She blogs at susiebright.com.

The Perils of the Hand-Sewn Gift

My mom once made me a remarkable dress for my 14th birthday. After modeling for her with a frozen smile, I covertly wadded the dress up in a ball and hid it in the knot of a tree a half a block away.

My birthday frock was Italian Swiss cotton, a lime and lemon print, with elaborate smocking on the bodice, and hand embroidery, which took Mommy two months to complete. An heirloom treasure, by any account.

It was 1972: a decade of hot pants, polyester shine, and sleek silhouettes. My dotted Swiss frock was adorned with puffed sleeves, a Peter Pan collar, and a hem that fell *two inches below my knees*. I looked like a doddering child from a *Father Knows Best* episode. If I wore that dress to school, I would've been beaten up, egged, TP'd, and left for dead in the girl's bathroom.

I tell you this tragic tale with a lesson in mind: it's a dicey proposition to make a hand-sewn gift. The levels of potential rejection, disillusionment, and incomprehension are hazards without parallel.

Clearly, the mother-daughter scenario is the most deadly. The daughter's anguish over puberty leads her to believe that anything her mother makes for her is designed to destroy her social life. She is probably right.

But what about more neutral territory? What if you want to craft a garment or bit of home decor for a dear friend? Won't they be charmed, pleased, in awe of the labor you put into art?

Not necessarily. People who don't sew (or knit or weave, etc.) have no earthly idea what goes into even a simple project. That's why they hand us their trousers to be altered and imagine it's a five-minute affair. They think little fairies come in with (free) needles, (free) thread, and magic cloth (that doesn't cost $10 a yard) to whip up cute dresses and jackets over the course of a sitcom or two.

In her famous yarn primer, *Stitch 'N Bitch* author Debbie Stoller took a hard line on knitting presents: she advised that you knit gifts exclusively for other knitters, since they are the only ones who will "grok" what you've put into your passion: the money, time, endurance, and invention.

So why do we all ignore this hard-won bit of advice? Because we're showoffs. We know modesty is supposed to go hand in hand with our steady stitches, but we yearn for people's jaws to drop open at our handiwork. We like making things for our beloveds and watching their hearts melt. We're sentimental fools who want only to be adored for our talents. *Is that too much to ask?*

Seeing a friend or family member wear your handmade clothes is like a musician hearing their song for the first time on the radio. It's a rush. Just imagine how a designer feels witnessing thousands of people influenced by a little decision she made one afternoon in a sewing room. We'd all like a little taste of that.

I have a few gift projects to suggest. These items do not rely on how many hours you spend making them, but rather the opposite: the hours your loved ones will spend wearing and using them.

Your family, both immediate and species-wide, spends about a third of their lives in bed. This is where you're going to insinuate yourself: in their blankets, their PJs, their bathrobes — even where they lay their heads at night.

Pillowcases are easily made and instantly treasured. The fabric prints you can find in flannel and cotton today are mind-boggling. If you have a friend who is into Buddhism, cats, and absinthe, there is very likely a print of that exact composite. Go to a site like fabricparadise.com, where you can put in a subject, like "vintage," "Chinese food," or "news headlines," and you will see fabrics that play the part.

Illustration by Melinda Beck

Pajamas and bathrobes are worn every night by happy campers who will not tear at the seams and demoralize you with questions like, "Does my ass look fat in this?" If all you know is that their favorite color is "blue," you can make them dream-worthy nightclothes of satin, flannel, silk, and soft cotton. A silky nightshirt is a luxury not soon forgotten.

Now that only the very wealthy can afford to turn their heat on, blankets are going to be more prized than ever. The materials home sewers can buy today are so plush: minky with a flannel back, fake fur or suede with a flannel back, polar fleece with a ... you get the idea. You don't need a pattern: just cut two pieces the same size and stitch them together. Put a cozy trim around the edge and you'll have a blankie so righteous it will inspire thumb sucking. You can make one of these in a couple of hours, and your darling daughter/son/lover/best mate will be besotted with it for the rest of their lives.

But what about the daytime? Is there any surefire gift you can sew that your recipient is guaranteed to wear outside, in view of an admiring public? There are two areas where you cannot go wrong: cold weather and babies.

Hats, as long as they are simple, like a watch cap or beret — or better yet, a *crown* — are always a hit.

Five-fingered gloves are a pain to sew — that's why they're so expensive to buy, because constructing those little finger compartments is not for the faint of heart. However, knitted or stretch-wear gauntlets are awesome, and a breeze to make. The forearm-sized tubes stop at the wrist or just before the fingers, sparing you any complexity. Make a thumbhole if you really want to be impressive.

Gauntlets have a special meaning to those who use keyboards in their daily lives. Everyone hates the feeling of a cold, hard keyboard first thing in the morning or on a chilly day. These soft protectors

We like making things for our beloveds and watching their hearts melt.

around your wrists and lower palms turn a Monday hangover into a soft landing.

I've saved the most endearing for last: baby clothes. To be specific, rompers. There will never be a time when anyone looks better in a romper than under the age of 18 months — but what a time it is!

First, you can stuff babies into anything, and they don't even know what's going on. They look fabulous in every color; they're stunning in a sack. For half a yard of fabric, you can make snap-up rompers in the most hilarious prints with outlandish buttons and trims, appealing only to their parents' egos.

The key to romper prep is this: buy snap tape, cotton tape that has embedded snaps every couple of inches, by the yard. You sew the tape onto the legs, and voila, you're finished.

New parents are insecure, trying to be perfect in a cruel and chaotic world. When you make a romper for their newborn, they unfold the little garment and cry out with delight. The Earth rights its axis, the sun gets a little skip in its step. They will treasure this little original for their children and their great-grandchildren. The babies will wiggle their impossibly tiny fingers and toes with life, stretching your romper to its limits — and you'll say to yourself, "Now this is what gift giving is all about." ✂

✚ Check out Susie's extensive resources list at craftzine.com/06/bright.

HANDMADE

Photography by Robin Lasser and Adrienne Pao

Pitch a Dress

Robin Lasser stands at the Mexico-California border fence, a watchful figure of incredible height in camouflage fatigues. She peers through binoculars and searches for illegals attempting to sneak over the line.

But Lasser, in life, is no vigilante. She's no border agent either. She's an assistant professor of art at San Jose State University who, with **Adrienne Pao**, a photographer and one of her former students, created a series of photographs and live exhibitions of wearable architecture called *Dress Tents*.

Ms. Homeland Security: Illegal Entry Dress Tent is one of these pieces of nomadic attire. It fits snugly into a bag and can be fully assembled and donned in a couple of hours. *Picnic Dress Tent* is another. It features Pao literally tethered to 50s-era female domesticity in a humongous red-and-white gingham number. "I thought it'd be amazing to deal with this idea of camping and the body and make it photographic," Pao says.

The pair dreamt up a suite of site-specific outfits, chose fabrics that worked with the landscapes, and got help from seamstresses in the Bay Area to construct the garments (sometimes using actual tents as scaffolding). On location, either Lasser or Pao modeled the duds while the other shot.

But a Dress Tent doesn't stop with a still. The artists designed and built elaborate inner sanctums within the structures to be experienced in a gallery. By ducking beneath *Security*'s skirt, crossing a border of sorts between public and private, visitors watch video of the scene on the other end of the binoculars.

"My desire is to experience life and then communicate it," Lasser says. "Some artists just want to speak to themselves. For me, it's always been important to make my art for the public."

While Dress Tents are meant to push buttons, they're also meant to be whimsical. Future tents will incorporate smart fabrics that change color with temperature, and one may involve live bees — thus, Lasser or Pao would become queen.

—*Megan Mansell Williams*

>> **Dress Tents:** robinlasser.com, adriennepao.com

Perfect Pair

Before Seattle-based jeweler, sculptor, and conceptual artist **Jana Brevick** set out to produce her series of Cat 5-compliant wedding rings, she did some research to see if anyone else was already making them. "The joke was so funny and obvious that I thought it'd already been done," she says.

It hadn't been done, so she raided the back stock bins at hardware stores to collect oversized male/female sets. She wanted the parts to be big enough to get the joke across and to highlight the sculptural aspects of the connectors.

Everchanging Ring, one of the artist's more popular projects, best exemplifies how Brevick strives for unity of form, function, and meaning. The 24-karat gold wedding band can be returned on an annual basis to be reshaped. More often than not, the owners wind up loving it as is and don't want it changed at all.

Brevick's ongoing exploration of outdated technology encompasses both wearable sculptural objects and large-scale art installations. *Tinker Tailor Jeweler Spy*, her 2006 exhibition at Soil Art Gallery, investigated the culture of post-9/11 surveillance.

"I didn't feel like I had any secrets anymore," Brevick says about the show's impetus. A 12"-high skyscraper was outfitted with a jumble of miniature sterling silver antennas while *Personal Top-Secret Password Printer* came with a tiny silver satellite dish. Along similar lines is the recent *Moving Target* series — necklace pendants in the shape of a bull's-eye. Brevick says she's interested in the "beautiful, classic design" and its implications about the hunter and hunted.

Brevick is currently researching how to incorporate Nixie tubes — glass tubes used to display neon numerals — into jewelry. "They're so enchanting because they glow and the scale lends itself to being worn," she said. However, she's run into a minor obstacle in terms of how to power them. "You can't wear that much battery pack on your back," she says. Doubtless, Brevick will devise an elegant solution, one that reckons with technology on its own terms.
—*Katie Kurtz*

>> **Brevick's Jewelry:** flickr.com/photos/janabrevick

Photograph by Roger Schreiber

Stitch House

Photograph by Alison Murray

At first glance there's nothing unusual about **Alison Murray**'s home in Bideford, South West England. There's a cozy living room with table and chairs. A bedroom with pillows and blankets. Eggs and bacon in a frying pan on the kitchen stove.

But this entire cottage, and everything in it, has been knitted by hand — the cupcakes on a plate, the cat curled on the bed, and every flower in the woolen garden blooming beside the 12-foot knitted trees. Not to mention the knitted teapot, cups and saucers, and portraits on the walls.

"I've always thought of knitting as art, more than just scarves and sweaters," says Murray, age 45, who works as a chaperone for child stars of film and TV when she's not stitching. "It's not just for grandmothers. I've always loved sculptural knitting, crafting giant ketchup bottles and mermaids. But I decided I wanted a bigger project."

Millions of stitches later, she has a life-sized gingerbread house comprising thousands of multicolored knitted squares hung on a metal frame. Knitted candies and cakes decorate the knitted roof and walls.

Murray launched her first oversized project in 2005, when she crafted a 25-foot-high Christmas tree to raise money for charity, with the help of friends: some 700 friends contributed thousands of knitted tree limbs.

Last year knitters from across America joined those in the U.K., Spain, and France to craft details for the gingerbread house. They stitched pet guinea pigs, saltwater taffy and gateaux, roof tiles, rugs, furniture, lollipops, and more than 2,500 gingerbread men, all mailed to Murray.

"I knitted for months myself, making a broom, logs of firewood, a cuckoo clock, and much more," she says. "It allowed children to get involved [by] knitting parts of the project, and best of all we are raising funds to help support children's hospitals."

The house is touring Britain through 2008, and Murray says, "It's changing people's attitudes to knitting. Now I'm planning next year's project: it'll be bigger than ever." —*Peter Sheridan*

≫ **More photos:** craftzine.com/06/handmade_house

Soft Power

"When I look out my window, I can see across to the Mexican side of the border," says **Margarita Cabrera** from her home in El Paso, Texas. Born in Mexico, she and her family immigrated to the United States when she was a child. The two cultures are certainly inspiring, but the primary influence for Cabrera's fanciful, soft sculptures lies right outside her window.

After moving to El Paso from New York, where she was studying art, Cabrera became interested in the lives of men and women toiling in factories along the U.S.-Mexico border. Though it's difficult to gain entry to these establishments, she managed to visit one. Her experience inspired a series of sculptures based on objects produced in the factory. Most of these are commonly used machines; Cabrera wanted to highlight the contributions of immigrant workers to familiar conveniences of everyday American life.

She handcrafts each object from vinyl, using industrial sewing machines and sometimes a needle and thread. "Vinyl is a substitute for something better," Cabrera explains, "but it's cheap and it's often used to cover surfaces. I wanted to use it in the opposite way, to expose everything."

Her process also works from the outside in: she takes extensive measurements and makes comprehensive drawings of each blender and coffee machine, bicycle and backpack, before creating her own version in vinyl. As a result, Cabrera has effectively invented her own method of pattern making.

Perhaps most ambitious — and certainly most dramatic — is a silver Hummer, made to scale and constructed from vinyl using her meticulous process. Each button and switch, door handle and window-pane is included. Even the interior structure is mirrored in layers and layers of sewn vinyl.

Cabrera chose this emblem of power and aggression because many of the Hummer's parts are made in Mexico, and because she sees these vehicles patrolling the border each day. The size of the project let her hire an assistant; Cabrera happily found Laura Vera, an unemployed factory worker, who continues to work in the studio today. —*Annie Buckley*

>> **More of Cabrera's Work:** margaritacabrera.com

BUSINESS REPLY MAIL
FIRST-CLASS MAIL   PERMIT NO 865   NORTH HOLLYWOOD CA

POSTAGE WILL BE PAID BY ADDRESSEE

NO POSTAGE
NECESSARY
IF MAILED
IN THE
UNITED STATES

Craft:

PO BOX 17046
NORTH HOLLYWOOD CA 91615-9588

Full Metal Skateboard

Photograph courtesy of Teofilo Cohen and Gabriel de la Mora

In contrast to the lightning pace of modern life, artist **Darío Escobar** uses a slow, hand-wrought process from centuries past to make his fun but luminous sculptures. Playing with conceptual borders — between old and new, high and low, religious and secular — Escobar enshrines contemporary objects like a skateboard, surfboard, or basketball backboard in shimmering metal, using gilding and silver embossing techniques from the colonial era of his native Guatemala.

The 12th century techniques lent baroque altars and candlesticks a sacred glow. Using them on everyday objects, Escobar draws humorous and insightful connections between devotion and consumerism.

His labor-intensive process produces amazing results, but it takes time. To complete the surfboard, for example, it took Escobar three months of full-time work with the help of four assistants.

To start with, he chooses the object by reflecting on symbolism, in particular from North American sports culture. Next he draws an elaborate design on silver, tin, or aluminum. The metal is then pounded to give form and volume to each curving line and elaborate scroll. Finally, the sheets are attached to the selected object. To give the surface its shine, Escobar brushes it with the same mixture of lemon and bicarbonate used by craftsmen long ago.

Escobar lives and works in Guatemala City, but his resplendent sculptures have been exhibited in the United States, Costa Rica, Mexico, and Ireland. Recently his work traveled to the Museum of Contemporary Art in Sydney, Australia, and to the exhibition *Poetics of the Handmade* curated by Alma Ruiz at the Museum of Contemporary Art in Los Angeles. The weight of Escobar's metal-clad sculptures makes transport tricky, and this exhibition brought five of them together at the same time.

Of the exhibition, Escobar says it was "fantastic" and explains that "to see so many of the works together in one room, in dialogue with the public and with other artists, was very emotional."

—Annie Buckley

≫ **Darío Escobar:** craftzine.com/go/escobar

Cathy Callahan
Old School

» Cathy Callahan is a crafter and window dresser who draws inspiration from vintage crafts. She blogs about 60s and 70s crafts at cathyofcalifornia.typepad.com.

The Craft of Casseroles

Casseroles were a staple when I was growing up in suburban Southern California during the 60s and 70s. They were touted in recipe books and women's magazines as an easy and economical way to make dinner for your family. My mom would always rather craft than cook, so making casseroles was a way she could use her crafty skills to whip up a quick dinner.

There is a basic formula to making a casserole that you can rework in countless combinations.

In my mom's 1971 *Betty Crocker's Recipe Card Library* (housed in a beautiful avocado and lime-green box) are 27 casserole recipes for such delights as Hamburger Pie, Garden Supper Casserole, Dinner in a Dish, Frank-Bean Bake, and Zippy Beef Casserole.

There is a basic formula to making a casserole that you can rework in countless combinations. Most recipes call for some type of meat combined with noodles, rice, or vegetables, which can be compared to your favorite craft supplies such as felt, pompoms, rickrack, etc. You'll need some kind of "glue" to hold it all together, like soup, ketchup, or sour cream. I like to think of the crunchy top (like bread crumbs, crispy onions, or chow mein noodles) as the glitter.

I felt drawn to the Zippy Beef Casserole recipe because it's made from many of the same ingredients my mom liked to use: ground beef, elbow macaroni, cream of mushroom soup, ketchup, cheddar cheese, green pepper, instant minced onion, and crushed potato chips. But I updated the recipe with healthier ingredients (well, except the corn chips). And just as you might do while following the directions for a craft project, feel free to increase or decrease ingredients to suit your taste, or add whatever else you think sounds good. ✖

RECIPE
1lb Soyrizo, crumbled and browned
8oz cooked organic macaroni
Two 15oz cans organic tomato sauce
½c chopped red onion
½c chopped bell pepper
1c shredded soy cheese
1c crushed corn chips

Preheat oven to 350°. Mix all ingredients (except corn chips) in an ungreased 2-quart casserole dish. Cover and bake for 40 minutes. Uncover, sprinkle with corn chips, and bake 5 minutes longer. Makes 4 to 6 servings.

Make sure to save some leftovers for lunch the next day so you'll have even more time to craft!

Repro-
depot
fabrics

Vintage reproduction and retro-themed textiles.
www.reprodepot.com

OUR FAVORITE
TRINKETS & TREASURES

1. Giving Tree

A masterpiece of design, Nick Foley's Pear Light is a delicious mix of art, technology, and fantasy. The tree is a charging station for the pluckable pear-shaped bulbs, which remain illuminated by ultrabright LEDs for up to an hour by themselves. craftzine.com/go/pearlight

2. Sweater Edition

Newsknitter is a "data visualization project," which sounds a bit dry, but meditation on the connection between the news and daily life. Internet news feeds are converted into visual patterns, which are turned into knitwear using a computerized knitting machine. casualdata.com/newsknitter

3. Pretty Yeti

The yeti has long been an object of fascination. But what does he do when he's not being abominable? Megan Whitmarsh has some ideas, and her charming retro-futuristic embroidered artworks show yetis scaling mountains, breakdancing, and rocking out to KISS.
tinyindustries.com

4. Windup Lamp

Form truly does follow function in this clever concept lamp. A windup spring powers the bulb; when the key returns to the starting position, the light turns off. Perfect for those who fall asleep with the lights on, or who have a penchant for visual jokes.
craftzine.com/go/windup

5. Quiltbert

Evil Mad Scientist Laboratories has done it again! This lap-sized quilt plays on the geometry of both classic tumbling block quilts and early video games. We love the color choices and appliquéd characters!
craftzine.com/go/quiltbert

6. Peep Shoes

A murmur went around the office over Hetty Rose's stunning handmade shoes. Combining vintage kimono fabrics with elegant shapes and fun details like keyholes in the toe, every woman we know wants a pair of these. hettyrose.co.uk/shoes

7. Ring of Fire

These gorgeous fire pits put a bit of class into the beach bonfire. The flames dance; the steel tarnishes with age. They can even be converted to propane, so you can turn them on or off at will. Toasting marshmallows has never been so fun. johntunger.com

8. Fairy Tales

Amy Earles doesn't make ordinary paper dolls: instead of just changing clothes, these turn into other-worldly wild things. Anyone who has ever loved the transforma-tive power of playing with paper dolls will be drawn to her work, which walks the uneasy line between beauty and terror. pushedunder.com

» SMOCKS THAT ROCK

A. Tanya Mauler: luckx8.blogspot.com

B. Esti Gerson: estigerson.com

C. Ruth Singer: www.ruthsinger.com

D. Roberta Taylor: thegoddess.ca

E. Amy Zink: poppyheart.blogspot.com

PRAIRIE GIRL APRON CONTEST

We were blown away by the wonderful submissions that came pouring in for our apron contest, inspired by *The Prairie Girl's Guide to Life*, out last fall from Taunton Press. We had almost 200 entries, and every single one was a testament to the fact that aprons are as relevant today as they were to Laura Ingalls Wilder. We were delighted by the beauty, utility, silliness, elegance, and fun of the wildly different aprons. Some were frilly half aprons, some were practical full-length aprons, others were matching mother-daughter sets, but they all made us want to cover up and get messy in the kitchen or craft room. Thanks to everyone who sent us photos of their aprons and shared their stories about making them; be sure to check out our Honorable Mentions at craftzine.com/go/aproncontest!

CRAFTER

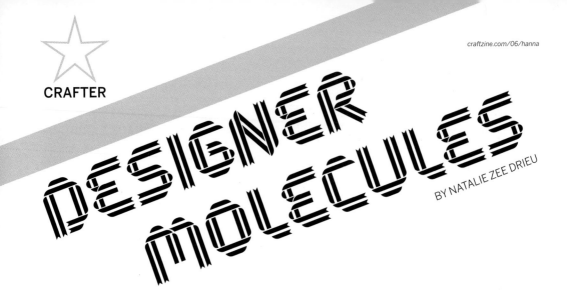

DESIGNER MOLECULES

BY NATALIE ZEE DRIEU

Biophysicist and jewelry designer Raven Hanna brings a scientific twist to crafts.

When it comes to science, San Francisco-based Raven Hanna knows what she's talking about. With a Ph.D. in molecular biophysics from Yale and post-doctorate work at U.C. Berkeley, the always-creative Hanna realized she didn't want to follow the typical scientist's path. After all, she used to make stuffed bacteria in grad school.

While researching neurotransmitters, Hanna found her jewelry calling. The serotonin molecule in a textbook illustration caught her eye and she wanted a necklace to represent it. After searching online, she realized they weren't sold anywhere, so she decided to make one herself.

The problem was, Hanna didn't actually know how to make jewelry. But thanks to the internet, she found a jewelry teacher on Craigslist to help her. "I showed him a drawing of the molecule attached to the chains and said, 'Teach me how to make this!'" she laughs.

In no time, Hanna's crafty hobby of making molecule jewelry became her number one passion and took most of her free time. When wearing her jewelry around town, she noticed that people who weren't scientists were intrigued by it. "What I was looking for, this 'visual science communication,' is right here in this hobby, and that's when I decided it would be neat to get it out there," she says.

Through the encouragement of friends, she made her hobby into a business, and Made with Molecules (madewithmolecules.com) was born. "Made with

Molecules is like 'made with love' but always accurate! Scientifically accurate!" exclaims Hanna.

From the stunning endorphin necklace to the delicate chocolate theobromine earrings, Hanna's jewelry is unique in the sense that she can showcase the beauty of it all first, letting the science sink in visually. "If the molecule isn't aesthetic, I'm not going to do it," Hanna explains.

To create her pieces, Hanna first finds a beautiful molecule and strips the design down to the basics so that it's graphically appealing. The finished CAD file is then sent to someone who prints it on a 3D laser printer in resin. Finally, the resin pieces are cast in silver and Hanna solders them together.

It wasn't long before CERN, the world's largest particle physics lab in Geneva, Switzerland, started knocking on her door. For two months in the spring of 2006, Hanna worked at CERN, along with their particle physicists, to make designs of subatomic particles. "It was the best job ever! Where do I go from here?" jokes Hanna. Inspired by the experience, today Hanna looks to diversify her work by exploring more in the particle physics realm, as well as going "bigger," into neurons and cells.

"Scientists devote their lives to what they study," explains Hanna. "They want some sort of beautiful thing to represent that to the world." Thanks to Raven Hanna, now they've got it. ✕

Natalie Zee Drieu is senior editor of CRAFT and writes for the CRAFT blog at craftzine.com.

Photograph by Gabriela Hasbun

SCIENTIFIC SILVER: Raven Hanna sports her lovely serotonin molecule necklace (see inset) at her jewelry-making table.

MADE WITH LOVE BY HANNAH

BY JENNY RYAN

Hannah Kopacz' world includes frisky gnomes, squirrel brooches, and a Cuckoo Cabin full of enchanted craftiness.

Upon visiting the website of Hannah Kopacz, madewithlovebyhannah.com, you might assume she lives a fairy-tale existence in an Alpine cottage somewhere, crafting the hours away with a songbird on her shoulder in a garden full of toadstools. You're not too far off the mark, only swap the songbird for three cats, two fish, and a grumpy bunny named Bucky.

Her garden does feature toadstools, but they're made of spray-painted concrete, and her cottage is a charmingly decorated shack she uses as a screen-printing studio. Also, she's based in sunny Los Angeles.

Kopacz got her start in sewing by making a terry-cloth bathrobe (complete with pompom fringe!) at age 6, and spent her teen years restyling vintage finds à la Molly Ringwald in *Pretty in Pink*. She then signed up for a high school silk-screening class as a way to meet cute punk boys, but discovered that she actually liked it — so much so that she ended up working in a screen-printing shop after graduation.

A customer offered her a job with his wholesale import clothing business, and by her mid-20s she was running her own clothing line. This was pre-internet, which made it a lot harder to earn a living as an independent designer.

She eventually moved cross-country from Massachusetts to L.A. and took a job working for a misses clothing line doing textile design for the mass market — think glittery snowman sweatshirts and the like. Despite the cornball imagery she

often found herself working on, the job gave her an excellent education in designing graphics and patterns, which she relished after spending a couple of short-lived semesters at Massachusetts College of Art and Design (MassArt) and Fashion Institute of Technology (FIT).

"School was not for me," Kopacz admits. "I just like to take a class here and there if I want to learn something hands-on that I can't learn from reading a book ... like welding."

Fortunately, once the urge to strike out on her own came over Kopacz yet again (and the web orders started rolling in), her employers allowed her to reduce her hours bit-by-bit until she was eventually working for herself.

Something that sets Hannah's clothing apart is that she really and truly has a hand in every step of the process. She designs the folksy-sweet patterns herself, screen-prints (and often hand-dyes) the fabrics in her Cuckoo Cabin, then stitches up the skirts, dresses, and tops that have made her line synonymous with crafty cuteness. This attention to detail is apparent when you wear a piece of her clothing, but Kopacz herself admits it's a bit of a stumbling block when it comes to growing her business — a concern many ambitious crafters share.

"I want to stay independent and handmade," she explains, "but I have a problem with wanting to do everything myself. Not just business-wise, but also fixing the car, working on the yard, you name it. That's my biggest problem right now: figuring out

Photography by Robyn Twomey

★ HANNAH'S WORKSHOP:
Fairy-tale-inspired skirts and
dresses come to life in Kopacz'
candy-colored sewing room.

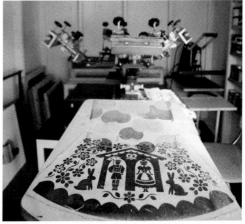

★ **ENCHANTED COTTAGE INDUSTRY: (Clockwise from top left) Gnomes and toadstools adorn the Black Forest-themed Schwarzwalder Skirt; Kopacz' infamous Cuckoo Cabin; silk-screened skirt panels in progress.**

some kind of place between growing and staying small. Is that even possible?"

Hannah's clothing is clearly well made, but what jumps out is just how fun it all is. Skirts are festooned with frisky gnomes, juicy green apples, candy-colored tulips, and retro sunflowers — some even feature removable squirrel brooches. With such playfulness, it's easy to see why Kopacz finds the actual screen-printing to be the most relaxing and enjoyable part of the design process.

"That folksy imagery really has a compelling sense of history for me; it gives me a feeling of nostalgia for a past I don't remember but wish I did," says Kopacz. "I always liked traditional folk handicrafts and clothing, things that were made by hand with love, and loved. That kind of stuff gives me a happy memory feeling, even if it's not my memory."

Kopacz' affection for the handmade is shared by many of her friends and family members (including her boyfriend's mom, who has her own page on

Hannah's website called Made with Love by Grandma, where the 80-something sells snail-shaped potholders and popsicle-stick purses). Her reverence for old-school crafting is also evident in her popular blog, Knick Knacks & Ric Rac, where she catalogs her thrift-store finds, home improvement projects, and endless sources of inspiration.

"I'll see something that tickles my fancy, some kind of cute doodad that will make me want to sketch out a new design," she says. "I have stacks and stacks of sketches — like ten years' worth — which I keep in case I suddenly run out of ideas."

But judging by what we've seen of Hannah Kopacz so far, that's just not likely. ✖

📷 See more images at craftzine.com/06/kopacz.

Jenny Ryan is an L.A.-based writer, crafter, and event organizer working on her first book, *Sew Darn Cute*, out next winter from St. Martin's Press. She drinks a *lot* of espresso.

Ulla-Maaria Mutanen
Linkages

Ulla-Maaria Mutanen lives in San Francisco and is CEO of Social Objects, Ltd., founder of Thinglink (thinglink.org), and author of the HobbyPrincess blog (hobbyprincess.com).

Play Time

Remember how full of enticing questions the world was when you were little? What if you could fly like a bird? Or, how could you breathe underwater? Many of us spent hours or even days building our own flying machines from materials we could find (umbrellas and a hair dryer in my case). So did Leonardo da Vinci, the greatest crafter of all time.

Da Vinci wasn't just a painter and sculptor. He was a scientist, mathematician, anatomist, musician, and architect. Most importantly, though, he was an unparalleled inventor and craftsman. His inventions included the helicopter, the submarine, and the ball bearing, just to name a few.

Recently, I had the chance to visit an exhibition showcasing reproductions of da Vinci's many inventions at the Metreon in San Francisco. As I drifted through the exhibition, I found myself wondering how it had been possible for one person to accomplish so much with so little.

His knowledge of physics was superficial, yet he managed to design an experimental helicopter. He had read less than a first-year medical student about physiology, yet he discovered arteriosclerosis. Where are the da Vincis of our day and age, I wondered. What is it that makes a person so creative?

Lev Vygotsky, one of the founders of modern psychology, had an interesting answer. He suggested creative accomplishments were not due to superior intelligence. Neither were they the product of high formal education. Rather, Vygotsky connected creativity with something deceptively simple: the ability to play. He considered play the most genuine and effective form of creative activity. "In play, a child is always above his average age, above his daily behavior; in play, it is as though he were a head taller than himself," Vygotsky wrote.

Play is open-ended. It is about improvisation, surprise, and switching roles — just the things our schools and workplaces are built to resist. We think problems today are so complicated that they're better left for buildings full of specialized scientists to solve. True enough, individuals can't master all knowledge like they could in da Vinci's day. But maybe our specialization is preventing us from seeing the big picture. Maybe it keeps us from asking the sorts of questions only children would ask.

Crafty questions trigger projects that, once we embark on them, make us smarter than we were before.

Craft is a form of play. It makes us ask those kinds of practical questions. "How can I make yarn?" "How can I grow my own food?" Crafty questions trigger projects that, once we embark on them, make us smarter than we were before.

The more interesting the question, the more motivated we are to solve it, and the more we learn by trying out different possible solutions. Crafters follow da Vinci's method. Working with the materials and knowledge they've got, they sometimes surprise with ingenious solutions.

The generation after us is faced with the most basic questions of all, those of survival. We are raising that generation now. Crafting brings potential solutions to smaller and bigger problems within our reach. More than being about academic knowledge, it's about a can-do attitude. When planning their curricula, schools would do well to remember da Vinci and the power of play. ✖

NEW YORK

BY DIANA ENG

Shop your heart out for all that's crafty in the Big Apple.

Whether you're a resident of NYC or a visitor, you'll find plenty of shops to explore in Manhattan. This borough has every store imaginable, with any material you may need for any craft. Here are a few fabulous places to shop: some famous, and some well-kept secrets.

M&J Trimming

1008 Sixth Avenue mjtrim.com

This is the famed, must-see trim store that you may recognize from Season 1 of *Project Runway*. When you walk through the door, you're overwhelmed with all the choices: ribbon, lace, appliqué, cording, buttons, feathers, purse handles, and closures. The staff is knowledgeable, helpful, and expert with the store's massive inventory. I had a wonderful chat with Auticia, who's worked at M&J for over 30 years with celebrity clients from movie stars to governors.

Food Match: You can "craft" for lunch at Craft (craftrestaurant. com), owned by famed *Top Chef* judge Tom Colicchio.

Toho Shoji

990 Sixth Avenue (one block from M&J) tohoshoji-ny.com

This jewelry supply store sells parts for your traditional projects and your wildest craft designs. They offer demonstrations periodically, so check online for a schedule. My favorite item was the new Free Metallico, a fine wire lace ribbon that's like stretchable chain maille, now being used for jewelry and flowers.

Food Match: Head a few blocks south to Koreatown for an authentic Korean meal, pastries, or frozen yogurt at Pinkberry (pinkberry.com). Be sure to try the secret topping, mochi!

N.Y. Elegant Fabrics

222 West 40th Street nyelegantfabrics.com

Although less than ten years old, this store has an enormous collection of fabrics, in mountains piled over ten bolts high. The owners travel everywhere looking for the most beautiful and also the most unique yardage. The most exquisite fabrics here can be priced at $200/yd plus.

Food Match: Head a few blocks east to the Bryant Park Café, which sits in the shadow of the N.Y. Public Library, and soak up the atmosphere looking out at the park. Or, if it's chilly, keep heading east to Grand Central Station and try the oysters at the famed Oyster Bar.

Pearl Paint

308 Canal Street pearlpaint.com

Located in Chinatown, this store has five floors of discounted art supplies. There are rooms for specialty papers and watercolors, walls of markers and paints, and shelves of instructional and blank books. Behind the main store are the Frame Shop and a Home Decor & Craft Center. They have a wonderful selection of color sample paints, not only the chips but also small jars for testing or using on a small project.

Food Match: Have dim sum (Chinese brunch) in one of the restaurants nearby. If you're veggie, play it safe at Vegetarian Dim Sum House (vegetariandshouse.com) on Pell Street.

Kiteya

464 Broome Street kiteyany.com

A favorite of mine is this beautiful Japanese shop; all items in the store, including the architecture, are made by Japanese craftsmen. A feast for the eyes and an inspirational experience, Kiteya's craft supplies include washi and origami papers, fabrics, ribbons, handmade glass beads, and scarves for wrapping your special gifts in traditional Japanese style. They also carry handcrafted purses, painstakingly created using a traditional technique of multicolored dyeing and gilding. They also have occasional demonstrations covering traditional Japanese crafts.

Food Match: Since you're in SoHo, have a drink and steak frites at Balthazar (balthazarny.com) and imagine you're in 1940s Paris. Afterward, stroll over to Sullivan Street and check out Purl SoHo for knitting supplies.

Diana Eng is a fashion designer who designs with technology. Known as the "fashion nerd" from *Project Runway: Season 2*, her interest in sewing began at an early age, when she created stuffed animals with her grandmother. populartransit.com

*De*CORRUGATED

BY ANNA DILEMNA

Frank Gehry popularized cardboard furniture in the 1970s, and now it's making a comeback.

Admit it. We've all had the cardboard box that came to stay, like that microwave box that you used as a "temporary" end table: eight months later it's buried under a pile of old magazines and overfilled ashtrays, a mysterious T-shirt wedged into one of the cracks.

Ten years later you might have classed it up a bit by draping it with fabric in an attempt to disguise its lowly, papery origins. After all, having furniture made from cardboard is decidedly not chic, right? Wrong! These days more and more eco-aware designers are turning to cardboard as a material that can be both sustainable and stylish.

Giles Miller (farmdesigns.co.uk) makes gorgeous patterns by exposing the rough edges of corrugated cardboard in his furniture, while companies such as Cardboard Design (cardboarddesign.com) highlight the versatility of the material by constructing furniture that expands and retracts, resulting in a dizzying array of amorphic yet functional items. Others, such as Dutch designer David Graas, make furniture that's built using its own shipping box as part of the final design.

Cardboard furniture isn't constricted solely to the world of high-end design, however. In Europe, particularly in France, it isn't at all uncommon to see people making and selling cardboard furniture out of their homes, and there's even a word in French, *cartonniste*, to describe a person who makes furniture from cardboard.

One of the most inspiring cartonnistes is Miss Julia (miss-julia.com), a graphic artist based in Marseille who incorporates the pictographs and typographies from the original boxes into her finished pieces.

Actually, the idea of making furniture out of cardboard isn't a new one. Perhaps most well known is the cardboard furniture designed by architect Frank Gehry in the 70s. Even back in the 60s, designers were experimenting with ways to use the abundant but unconventional material.

Designer Peter Murdoch created a popular line of cardboard furniture specifically for kids, which was sold at Bloomingdale's and mentioned in high-profile publications such as *Time* magazine. At the time, the furniture was seen as a novelty, and its easy disposability was more of an attraction than its ecological friendliness.

After all, this was the decade in which people were running around in paper dresses designed to be thrown out after only a few wears. The popularity of cardboard furniture died out several years later, however, and it was largely forgotten until recently, when designers began to revisit the idea — this time with an environmental perspective in mind.

Furniture made from cardboard can be surprisingly strong, holding up to several hundred pounds. Nevertheless, we're still left with a few concerns. Like what if you become over-animated while drinking red wine, resulting in a splashy accident? Or what if you're a smoker? An ashtray perched atop a table constructed of paper products just seems somehow, well, potentially catastrophic.

Makers of cardboard furniture say that these are valid concerns, although there are products to make the furniture more waterproof and less flammable.

Curiously, several designers who work with cardboard seem to feel that its fleeting nature is an integral part of its beauty, that to try and make it permanent would be defeating its point to begin with. Fans of the furniture feel that it's worth the risks. After all, they're paying for a design that's both ingenious and environmentally conscious,

Photograph by Rolf Kueng

Several designers who work with cardboard feel that its fleeting nature is an integral part of its beauty.

» *Foldschool's Nicola Enrico Stäubli takes a break on one of his cardboard stools.*

Clockwise from top left: *Rien Ne Peut* desk by cartonniste Miss Julia; Miss Julia's *1 2 3* pops with colorful graphics; *This Side Up* by David Graas; *Don't Spill Your Coffee Table* by David Graas.

not to mention providing guests with a good conversational centerpiece for many a red wine-less cocktail party to come.

Swiss designer Nicola Enrico Stäubli decided to skip the red wine and cigarettes crowd altogether and focus instead on the grape juice-swilling crowd. Currently, Stäubli's company Foldschool (foldschool.com) offers free designs for a stool, a chair, and a rocker, all geared toward children under 8 years old.

Oh, and another thing — Foldschool doesn't make the furniture for you. Instead, they tell you how to put it together yourself. Stäubli emphasizes that the process of crafting one's own furniture is an integral part of Foldschool's concept, and thanks to their downloadable patterns and a few readily available materials, we can whip up our own cardboardy furnishings in a matter of hours. Not only that, kids (and their crafty parents) can also further decorate the furniture, thus encouraging a multi-dimensional sense of craftsmanship and creativity.

In the end, whether we buy it or make it ourselves, cardboard furniture is more than just the latest gimmick. In a world of mass consumerism, it makes especially good sense to have furniture that can be produced, and disposed of, with little or no harm to the environment. If you'd like to become a carton-niste yourself, check out the fun tutorial (*page 94*) on how to build a chair from Foldschool!

Anna Dilemna is a doll maker and writer who has lived in New York City, Santiago, and Tokyo. Currently, she lives in Switzerland and eats lots of cheese. annadilemna.typepad.com

Craft and
COPYRIGHT

BY WENDY SELTZER

Protect your rights as creator and remixer.

Craft, meet copyright. You've seen the recording industry's file-sharing lawsuits but think copyright has nothing to do with you, right? After all, you're into knits, not bits. Well, sometimes you're right, but sometimes the lumbering giant of the law gets interested in crafts too, and the law, or proposed changes to it, could imperil your hobbies.

Needlepoint designers have been infiltrating exchange groups to stop the uncompensated sharing of patterns; eBay sellers face takedowns when they advertise their handiwork for sale; and fashion designers are lobbying Congress to extend copyright protection to fashion designs. What's a crafter to do?

Copyright and craft have an ambivalent relationship. Copyright is designed to "promote the progress of science and useful arts" by giving authors (and artists) a limited-time monopoly on their works. On the one hand, crafters are artists who may benefit from copyright's power to bar others from copying. Yet on the other, craft may build upon found objects or others' designs; artisans have always learned their trade by copying their predecessors, picking up a pen, brush, or chisel first to imitate, then to reinvent. Too strict an application of copyright may stifle the very creativity it is meant to promote.

To temper that threat, copyright exceptions are supposed to give leeway for creative reuse. While copyright limits copying of expression, it doesn't cover methods, functions, ideas, or *useful articles*.

The proportions in a recipe, steps for creating a particular type of stitch, concept of a "caution tape" scarf, and shape of a dress are all fair game. You're free to take any of these as building blocks for your own creations. Further, even copying of expression may be *fair use* for purposes such as criticism, commentary, or educational use. Crocheting a pop art "replica" of a purse or piece of jewelry fairly puts it in a new light rather than substituting for it. *First sale* lets you reuse physical items, like bolts of fabric you've bought, even if they include copyrighted expression.

But these exceptions don't always stop copyright claims, as Tom Forsythe found when he photographed Barbie wrapped in enchiladas and blended into margaritas. Mattel sued Forsythe for copyright infringement, arguing that the photos "reproduced" the Barbie image. It took years of litigation for Forsythe to vindicate his free speech defense: the use was fair as commentary on the dolls' objectification of women, and not infringement: the pictures would hardly replace the purchase of another doll for the Barbie mansion. In the end, Forsythe won a million-dollar judgment against Mattel.

Where do you stand if protracted litigation isn't your cup of tea?

Your artistic works are copyrighted upon creation, as soon as they're "fixed in a tangible medium of expression." If you do nothing further, the law forbids others from copying that goes beyond fair use. Readers can't take the pattern and detailed descriptions you've posted and copy them verbatim, but can they make and sell the craft described? That depends on the copyright in the crafted object: a richly patterned sweater's surface design could be copyright-protected, but its shape would not be. Further, if you've published a pattern, readers

probably get an implied license at least to make the craft from the pattern. That means, too, that when you're on the other side — using someone else's patterns — you're free to take uncopyrightable methods and useful articles, but you're limited in taking full-blown expression.

Instead of restriction, you might want to encourage greater reuse of your crafts through copyright. In that case, you might consider Creative Commons

> *Artisans have always learned their trade by copying their predecessors, picking up a pen, brush, or chisel first to imitate, then to reinvent.*

licenses, a set of badges and license terms to permit some copying. With the Share Alike license, for example, you invite people to modify your crafts and instructions so long as they acknowledge your work and share their results in the same way. Imagine sewing a quilt from Share Alike squares: each would be freely usable by anyone who contributes alterations back to the common pool.

Finally, if you're sharing your crafts online, you've probably run across (if not into) the Digital Millennium Copyright Act (DMCA) This 1998 law encourages internet service providers to respond to claims of users' copyright infringement by "expeditiously" taking down the complained-of material. Many copyright claimants thus send complaints to ISPs rather than to their users, and the service providers take down pages without investigating whether they infringe.

As a poster, you can counter-notify, but your pages will go back up only after a legally mandated delay. While a DMCA complaint might be appropriate against mass distribution of others' needlepoint designs, the takedown and delay will hurt lawful use if it targets the crafts you've made and photographed to sell on eBay.

So when fashion designers petition Congress to make their patterns copyrightable, they not only push aside creative reinvention, they open a new door for copyright-based threats. Yet the field has seen great creativity without copyright's incentives — the drive to stay ahead of copyists may even be good for the fashion cycle, while adding more copyright would put a thicket of licensing in the way of creative re-styling. As both creators and remixers, crafters should insist on balance in copyright law. ✂

Coming in CRAFT, Volume 07: Part Two of Seltzer's article, which will discuss craft trademark, publicity rights, and related areas of the law.

Wendy Seltzer is a fellow with Harvard's Berkman Center for Internet & Society and a visiting professor at Northeastern Law School. She leads the Chilling Effects Clearinghouse (chillingeffects.org).

Craft to play, or playfully craft! Just for the fun of it ...

Sew to juggle. Build to thumb a tune. Design to color a book of special moments. Solder wires to swivel a sparkly hula hoop. And knit to play with a plushie (or simply cuddle). The following pages are all about amusement, but we don't know which is more fun — crafting these projects, or playing with them afterward.

THUMB PIANO

Gather odd objects at home to make a musical lamellaphone. **BY RP COLLIER**

The thumb piano, known as a kalimba, mbira, and by many other names, is a lamellaphone that uses prongs called tongues, keys, or tines that you pluck to generate acoustic vibrations. The length of the tine determines the pitch.

Generally, the thumb piano uses some kind of mechanism as an anchor that puts a great deal of pressure over the tines and across 2 bridges, leaving the free lengths of the tines room to vibrate. The tines are usually of the same material and gauge (thickness) to ensure that the pressure is distributed equally, holding everything in place and in tune.

The method shown here is simplified and wonderfully versatile. It allows the use of more fragile, delicate, and unusual materials for the body of the instrument, and it provides a way to use oddly shaped tines of different materials while at the same time permitting the tines to be swapped out and tuned with ease.

I've included 2 materials lists: a generic list and one that is specific to the salad bowl kalimba shown here. Experiment, explore, and find configurations that work for you.

MATERIALS

» **Grounding bar** from the electrical section of a hardware store

» **Piano body** Examples here include a salad bowl, cigar box lid, wooden box, and aluminum block. You can use almost anything that's easy to hold and strong enough to withstand the fastening of a grounding bar and possibly a shim. Hollow or thin materials are good sound resonators; if your chosen body material doesn't resonate well, attach a resonator.

» **Shim (if needed)** can be a chunk of wood, metal, or plastic, ⅜" thick or thicker

» **Fasteners** such as hex screws, machine screws, wood screws, or nails

» **Tines** from a material firm enough to vibrate when plucked, up to ¼" wide: hairpins, wire, bicycle spokes, umbrella ribs, teriyaki skewers, knitting needles, street sweeper bristles, etc.

FOR A SALAD BOWL THUMB PIANO:

» **Grounding bar, 4¾" long** from the electrical section of a hardware store

» **Wooden salad bowl**

» **⅜" hardwood square dowel**

» **Spring steel, .032" thick × ⅛" wide, 60" long** from your local industrial steel distributor, trimmed to various lengths from 2" minimum to 6" maximum

» **#8 wood screws, 1¼" long (3)**

TOOLS

» **Hacksaw** to trim tines and, if desired, the shim. A hammer can be used instead of a saw to trim spring steel tines — clamp the tine in a vise and strike to bend it until it breaks. Wear eye protection!

» **Hand drill**

» **Drill bit** up to ¼"

» **Screwdrivers** flat blade or Robertson bit for the grounding bar, and whatever type is needed for your chosen fasteners (including hex key)

Photography by RP Collier

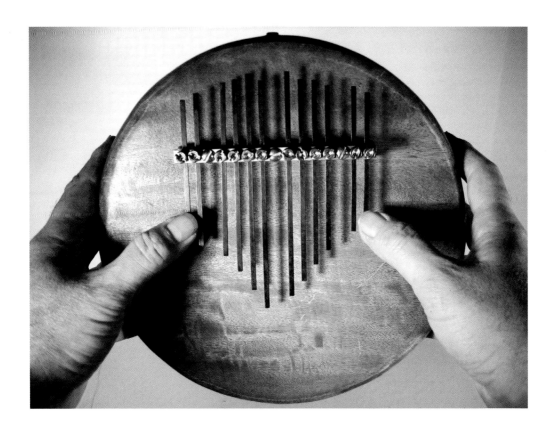

START »

1. **FASTEN THE GROUNDING BAR TO THE BODY OF YOUR INSTRUMENT**

The grounding bar is used by electricians to ground house circuit wires. It comes in various lengths and can be found in most local hardware stores or builder/contractor supply centers. The empty slots (2, 3, or more) come drilled all the way through — this is where fasteners can be used to attach the bar to something. But you may need to drill through if your slots aren't in the perfect places.

To anchor the grounding bar, simply make 3 holes with a hand drill into the surface you've chosen to be the body of the instrument. The screws shown in the bottom photo are hex head 10-32 machine screws (smaller and different types of machine screws could be used) secured with T-nuts, speed nuts, or standard nuts with lock washers and fender washers. If screwing into metal, you can use a tap to thread the holes.

If you're going to mount the bar on wood or thin metal such as a tin can, you may need only a hammer and nail to make the 3 holes. With wood, just use wood screws or something similar. Nails alone might possibly do the job with a bit of wood glue — start the holes with a nail, and add a bit of glue to the holes before driving them firmly. Heavy-duty epoxy, riveting, welding, or even slotting a surface with a milling machine or router are some other ways to anchor the bar.

2. ADD SHIMS, IF NECESSARY

The tines need room to vibrate, so depending on the type of surface chosen and the way the bar is mounted, you may need to lift the grounding bar up off the instrument body using a shim. This just requires 3 more holes using the grounding bar as a template.

The top photo shows shims made of ⅜" steel bar and wood square dowels. Plastic, clay, Bondo, Rock Hard Water Putty, or other materials could be used. The shims pictured are trimmed and clean, but they could be made of scraps, rough and with irregular edges, as long as the thickness is consistent.

The grounding bar provides a way to hold the tines using easily adjustable setscrews. The bottom photo shows the bar on a shim with the screw slots opened. You need a regular flat blade, standard tip screwdriver, or a driver with a Robertson bit.

3. ADD THE TINES

The tine can be anything that will vibrate and that will fit the hole. This photo shows a blue tempered spring steel tine. Crank the screw down tight to anchor the tine. This grounding bar can hold 12.

Metal tines can be bent away from the instrument to give more vibration room, which makes it easier to play.

TINE TIME

This image shows a grounding bar mounted on a small wooden crate from a thrift store, demonstrating what's great about this method: you can use tines in a variety of shapes, sizes, and materials at the same time.

These tines are made of (from left to right): blue tempered spring steel, hairpin, street sweeper bristle, unknown steel lattice debris, electrician's snake, knitting needle, street sweeper bristle, bicycle spoke, spring steel, umbrella rib, plastic hobby/craft brush, and plain steel wire with the end splayed by hammering.

The length of a tine determines its pitch. To tune a tine, loosen its screw, scoot it forward or backward a bit, retighten, and plunk.

◼ You can watch a video of this very roughly tuned thumb piano (shown at left) at craftzine.com/go/thumbpiano.

FINAL THOUGHTS

If you use a body that has a lip or an edge, like a wooden box or desk drawer, the tines are free to vibrate over the hollow of the receptacle, so a shim isn't necessary.

The inside of a cigar box lid can provide a shallow receptacle that fits well in the hands. Again, no shim is necessary. The tines shown at right are bamboo teriyaki skewers.

Below is an example of the grounding bar used on unusual materials but in a conventional way. The tines are spring steel and uniform across the span. The body is aluminum, a ¾"-thick block, and there is an aluminum shim.

I wanted to make something sleek that looks machined, but in actuality I just used a cheap, much-abused drill press. I used a tap to thread the anchor screw holes, putting the tap in the drill press and turning the chuck by hand.

Surprisingly, the thing is so heavy that a hollow door on sawhorses makes a good resonator for the instrument.

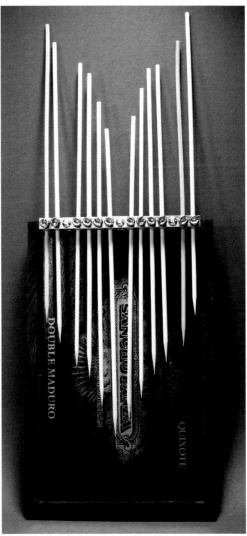

RP Collier is a visual artist, sound artist, and musician currently working in Portland, Ore.

MODERN PLAYSCAPE

Didi Dunphy transforms galleries into grown-up playgrounds with her colorful skateboards and adult-sized swings. **BY GARTH JOHNSON**

Didi Dunphy wants you to play with art. She blurs the lines between craft, art, and design with her candy-colored vinyl swings, teeter-totters, rockers, and indoor skateboards.

Her artwork bristles with stored energy that can only be unleashed when viewers leave their adult inhibitions behind and climb aboard. The objets d'art that Dunphy creates for her Modern Convenience line aren't merely inviting — they defy spectators not to participate.

For her recent solo exhibition called *Recess Playscape*, at the Atlanta Contemporary Art Center, Dunphy transformed a stark white gallery into a literal playground, complete with playground monitors armed with whistles. Crowds of teenagers vied with middle-aged museum-goers for a turn in the Skate area, where various Inside Skateboards decorated with padded vinyl and embroidered automotive pinstriping were lined up. The white wall of the gallery was blank except for one instruction: skate.

The main gallery area was reserved for Modern Convenience's line of adult-sized swings. Nine padded swings hung from industrial steel beams on plastic-covered chains. The swings were the focus of the room, which was accented with minimal vinyl polka dots on the floor. The tassels that hung from each swing added to the decadence, making them a hybrid of modern and rococo. A third gallery contained mysterious rockers that allowed riders to shimmy, twist, and invent their own movements.

Every project Dunphy undertakes is accomplished with her signature design sensibility, combining a minimalist aesthetic with an abundance of charm, warmth, and wit. In graduate school, she rebelled against the orthodoxy of male-dominated modernist painting by creating hard-edged geometric canvases

that referenced quilts and contained zippers, hems, and other trappings of domesticity.

"I sat down in my studio and tried to self-evaluate the role of a female studio artist," said Dunphy. Rather than deny the existence of gender roles and inequities, her work probes the sore spots with a humorous bedside manner.

The geometric works were followed by a series of tie-dyed paintings that ranged from minimal and monochromatic to canvases that looked like Jerry Garcia exploded on them. As a finishing touch, the tie-dyed pieces were covered with a layer of shiny varnish to lend an air of art-world authority.

Dunphy also created a massive body of cross-stitch samplers based on the stark, geometric paintings of Piet Mondrian, Ad Reinhardt, Frank Stella, and others. Rather than copy the paintings directly, she created her own patterns based on their styles. As a true pioneer of the DIY movement, she then offered the patterns for free on her website, so crafty fans of modern art could make their own Ellsworth Kelly aprons and Kenneth Noland placemats. Never before has the modernist grid been so ... huggable!

Abstract artist Barnett Newman said that sculpture is what you bump into when you back away from a painting to get a better look. Dunphy decided to create upholstered sculpture that would be a pleasure to bump into. Her oversized vinyl building blocks were sent to galleries, where curators and installers got to decide how they'd be set up, thus becoming artistic collaborators.

These sculptures spawned her current body of work: Modern Convenience's skateboards are pieces of sculpture you can ride. The genius of Modern Convenience is that the objects are equally at home

swing

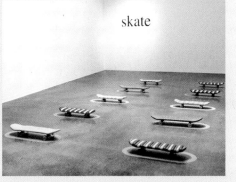

skate

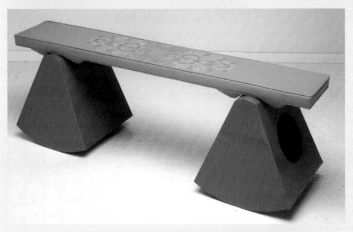

ARTFUL PLAY: Didi Dunphy's *Playscape* exhibition at the Atlanta Contemporary Art Center invited museum-goers to play with her interactive, color-popping art. In the Swing room she hung nine padded swings, each a different color of the rainbow. In the Skate room, vinyl-padded skateboards enticed people of all ages to take a ride. Other pieces included Dunphy's gliding bench, or "joggling board."

DUNPHY'S ARTWORK BRISTLES WITH STORED ENERGY THAT CAN ONLY BE UNLEASHED WHEN VIEWERS LEAVE THEIR ADULT INHIBITIONS BEHIND AND CLIMB ABOARD.

LEFT: Dunphy poses with her boards. RIGHT: This red aluminum bench, called *Kissing Jim*, is built for two. Its side-by-side, opposite-facing seating promotes "relaxing cheek to cheek."

in an art museum or in a private home. It's only when the objects are used, however, that they fully realize their potential as fine art.

Dunphy lives and works in Athens, Ga., which is better known for R.E.M. and rabid football fans than as a hotbed of modern design. It's her aim to change that through Athens Design Development (ADD), a coalition of like-minded designers and artists dedicated to bettering their city through innovative design. Their first two projects, bright yellow bus-shaped bus stop shelters and flower-shaped cigarette butt receptacles, were just unveiled. ADD is also sharing its expertise through a design directory that will help local artists, crafters, architects, and other designers find resources such as fabricators and materials.

Play is the unifying factor in Dunphy's work. "I'm currently exploring [Swiss philosopher] Jean Piaget's theory of cognitive play," she says. By letting viewers of all ages interact with her art, Dunphy

makes the realms of art and design accessible to a larger audience. As an artist, she is true to her singular vision, which uses seductive materials, sleek forms, and irresistible function to draw the spectator into a collaborative relationship.

As a brand, Modern Convenience injects much-needed playfulness into the hard-edged world of modern design. As art, Modern Convenience irresistibly invites your participation.

➕ Dunphy's Modern Convenience line: modernconvenience.com

Athens Design Development: add411.org

Garth Johnson is a designer, educator, and rogue crafter who lives in Atlanta. His website, extremecraft.com, is a compendium of craft masquerading as art, art masquerading as craft, and craft extending its middle finger.

WHICH CAME FIRST?

Explore the age-old question with this clever, knitted, reversible chicken-and-egg toy. **BY ANNA HRACHOVEC**

Photograph by Garry McLeod

It's a question for the ages, and now you can visualize this timeless conundrum with a most philosophical knitted toy — a reversible chicken and egg! Knitting and toys go together very well. The three-dimensional effect of knitting in the round makes for a free-standing, huggable new friend, and some simple assembly techniques transform it into an interactive toy.

When you're feeling confused about something, you can just play with your chicken and egg buddies and imagine what it's like for them!

Anna Hrachovec is a toy-crazy knitting designer living in New York. Her unusual patterns can be found at her website, mochimochiland.com

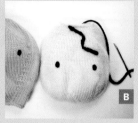

Fig. A: The eggshell and chicken's body parts before they are felted and stitched together. Fig. B: Features should be embroidered on the chicken and the eggshell before assembling the pieces. Fig. C: Before attaching the eggshell, stuff the legs and sew them onto the chicken, along with the unstuffed wings and beak, using a mattress stitch. Fig. D: Before stitching the egg and chicken together, stuff lightly between the 2 layers to add structure, but leave enough space to turn the toy inside out. Fig. E: Time to pop the chicken!

MATERIALS

» **Feltable, light, worsted-weight 100% wool yarn** in white (109yds), yellow (109yds), and orange (30yds)
» **Set of 7" size 5 double-pointed needles**
» **Tapestry needle**
» **Black embroidery thread and needle and/or small amount of black yarn**
» **Poly-fil** or other fiberfill stuffing
» **Standard washer and dryer** for felting
» **Scissors**

NOTE: Basic pattern techniques in this project include knitting in the round, I-cord, and felting, plus some simple sewing and embroidery. The finished size is about 5½" tall.

START »

1. Knit the eggshell and the chicken body.

The shell of the egg and the body of the chicken are identical, except for the colors you'll use. Use white yarn for the egg, then repeat the pattern in yellow for the chicken's body.

CO 32 sts onto 3 dpns and join in a rnd.
Unless noted below, knit all sts.
Rnd 1: [kfb, k7] to end
Rnd 3: [kfb, k8] to end
Rnd 5: [kfb, k9] to end
Rnd 7: [kfb, k10] to end
Rnd 9: [kfb, k11] to end
Rnd 12: [kfb, k12] to end
Rnd 15: [kfb, k13] to end
Rnd 18: [kfb, k14] to end
Rnd 21: [kfb, k15] to end
Rnd 24: [kfb, k16] to end
Rnd 27: [kfb, k17] to end
Rnd 31: [kfb, k18] to end
Rnd 35: [kfb, k19] to end (84 sts)

Photography by Anna Hrachovec

Rnd 41: [k2tog, k10] to end
Rnd 43: [k2tog, k9] to end
Rnd 45: [k2tog, k8] to end
Rnd 47: [k2tog, k7] to end
Rnd 49: [k2tog, k6] to end
Rnd 51: [k2tog, k5] to end
Rnd 53: [k2tog, k4] to end
Rnd 55: [k2tog, k3] to end
Rnd 57: [k2tog, k2] to end
Rnd 59: [k2tog, k1] to end
Rnd 60: [k2tog] to end (7 sts)
Cut yarn and draw the tail through
the remaining 7 sts.

2. Knit the chicken parts.

» Beak
With orange yarn, CO 10 sts onto 3 dpns
and join in a rnd.
Knit 4 rnds.
Next rnd: [k2tog] to end
Cut yarn and pull the tail through 5 sts.

» Wings (2)
With yellow yarn, CO 16 sts onto 3 dpns
and join in a rnd.
Unless noted below, knit all sts.
Rnd 2: kfb, k6, [kfb] twice, k6, kfb
Rnd 4: kfb, k8, [kfb] twice, k8, kfb
Rnd 6: kfb, k10, [kfb] twice, k10, kfb
Rnd 9: kfb, k12, [kfb] twice, k12, kfb (32 sts)
Rnd 12: k2tog, k12, [k2tog] twice, k12, k2tog
Rnd 14: k2tog, k10, [k2tog] twice, k10, k2tog
Rnd 16: [k2tog] twice, k4, [k2tog] 4 times, k4,
[k2tog] twice (16 sts)
Rnd 18: [k2tog] to end (8 sts)
Cut yarn and draw through sts.

» Legs (2)
With yellow yarn, CO 16 sts onto 3 dpns
and join in a rnd.
Unless noted below, knit all sts.
Rnd 2: [kfb, k3] to end (20 sts)
Rnd 5: [k2tog, k3] to end
Rnd 7: [k2tog, k2] to end
Rnd 9: [k2tog, k1] to end

Switch to orange yarn and knit 10 rnds.

Working in sections, divide your sts into 3 toes:
First toe: k2tog, k1. Work these 2 sts on your right nee-
dle in 4 rows of I-cord. Cut yarn and pull through sts.
Second toe: Reattach yarn to the next st, and k2.

Work these 2 sts in 4 rows of I-cord, cut yarn,
and pull through sts.
Third toe: Reattach yarn to the next st, k1, k2tog.
Work these 2 sts in 4 rows of I-cord, cut yarn,
and pull through sts.

3. Felt everything.

Weave in any loose ends, and lightly felt all pieces
by running them through a washer and dryer. I recommend felting everything in a lingerie bag, so you
don't lose any small pieces, and checking on the
felting while it's in the dryer to avoid over-felting.

If your pieces felt too tightly, the toy will be harder
to turn inside out, and some stitch definition will be
helpful when you sew everything together.

4. Embroider the features.

Using the photo as a guide, embroider eyes on
the chicken and the egg, with either embroidery
thread or black yarn. (I used embroidery thread for
the eyes and black yarn for the cracked shell.) The
tops of the chicken and the egg are opposite — the
top of the chicken is the closed end, and the top of
the egg is the open end.

Embroider the egg's crack as a thick zigzag line
(Figure B).

5. Sew on the chicken parts.

Without stuffing them, sew the CO edges of the
beak and the wings to the chicken using a mattress
stitch. Stuff the legs and sew them on at an angle,
again using a mattress stitch (Figure C).

6. Join the chicken and the egg.

Turn the egg inside out and stuff it inside the
chicken, with the egg's eyes lining up in roughly
the same place as the chicken's eyes. Stuff lightly
between the layers with fiberfill stuffing (Figure D).
The chicken shouldn't look like a withered balloon,
but you also need to leave room for turning the toy
inside out.

Hold the pieces in place and sew up the open
ends using a mattress stitch. Because of the nature
of this stitch, you should be able to use either yellow or white yarn without it showing in the seam.

Once sewn together, you should be able to pop
the chicken and egg out of one another by pushing in the closed end of each (Figure E). Doing this
a few times will loosen up the stitches a little and
make it gradually easier to turn inside out.

Time to cuddle, ponder, or play with your newly
hatched creation!

COLOR YOUR WORLD

Create coloring books in lieu of scrapbooks with your next batch of photos.

BY SUMMER BLOCK KUMAR

In the age of digital cameras, it's not uncommon to come home from vacation with hundreds, even thousands, of photos. Instead of asking all your friends to sit through a slideshow, try this new way to share your trip highlights.

Turning your vacation photos — or any digital images — into a themed coloring book creates an easy souvenir gift for your friends or travel companions. Bundle your outlined adventures together with crayons or colored pencils, and observe whether your friends are the type that color within the lines or go their own way. Or give children the coloring books in advance as a sneak preview of their vacation destination.

Images that work best have strong, clean lines, simple geometric shapes, and high contrast. Architectural photos make great coloring book pages, while human portraits might need a little more tweaking.

MATERIALS
- » Computer
- » Adobe Photoshop software
- » Digital photos
- » Color printer
- » Acid-free, heavy-stock paper
- » Binding machine
- » Crayons or colored pencils (optional)

Summer Block Kumar is a writer and contributor to artnet, *Alarm*, the *San Francisco Chronicle*, *Newsweek* China edition, *Small Spiral Notebook*, *Identity Theory*, and many other publications. Her work can be found at summerblock.com.

Photography by Dev Kumar

START »

1. OPEN YOUR IMAGE IN PHOTOSHOP
Make sure you have a backup copy before you begin.

2. CREATE A DUPLICATE LAYER
Choose Layer ⇒ Duplicate Layer.

3. CREATE AN IMAGE OUTLINE
Make sure your default ink color is set to black. Choose Filter ⇒ Sketch ⇒ Photocopy. You can adjust the levels of detail and darkness until you're pleased with the image. The image here uses Detail 4 and Darkness 10.

4. ADJUST LEVELS
To fine-tune your image, choose Image ⇒ Adjustments ⇒ Curves. You can also use the Lasso tool to adjust portions of the image that are lighter or darker than the rest. When you're satisfied with your picture, save the results as a JPEG file.

5. CREATE MARGINS AND CAPTIONS (OPTIONAL)
If you'd like to insert captions into your book (see photo 7), use Image ⇒ Image Size and Image ⇒ Canvas Size to change the position of your image on the page. Use the Text tool to write captions.

6. CREATE A COVER PAGE
You can add a full-color title page, or use one of your black-and-white outlines as the cover.

7. PRINT, BIND, AND BUNDLE
Choose File ⇒ Page Setup to select paper size. Print the coloring book pages in black and white, and the cover page in color (if you choose). For the best results, use high-quality, acid-free paper. Bind the book, and bundle it with boxes of crayons, colored pencils, or markers if it's going to be a gift.

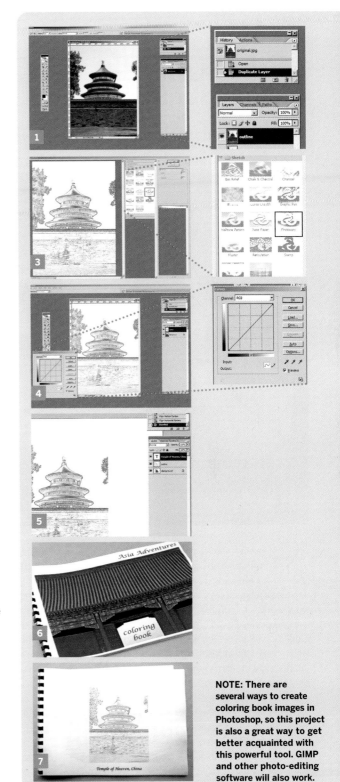

NOTE: There are several ways to create coloring book images in Photoshop, so this project is also a great way to get better acquainted with this powerful tool. GIMP and other photo-editing software will also work.

OTEDAMA

Make a set of Japanese juggling toys. **BY DIANE GILLELAND**

Need to improve your hand-eye coordination? Take up juggling. And make it crafty by whipping up a set of these soft, colorful Japanese juggling toys. All you need are some fabric scraps and a handful of dried beans or rice.

The Japanese word *otedama* refers to a variety of juggling games, played with small handmade toys, which originated in Japan way back in the 9th century. Interestingly, otedama games were historically played only by women and girls, who often juggled together in groups while singing otedama songs.

Otedama reached the height of its popularity after World War II, when other toys were scarce in Japan. Otedama could be easily sewn together from scraps of cloth, and filled with adzuki beans. In fact, parents in wartime Japan sometimes smuggled extra food to their children at school inside the otedama.

Otedama games, and the songs that accompanied them, were passed orally from mothers to daughters for hundreds of years, but today there's little record of the otedama tradition. The term has, however, become a more general name for juggling in modern-day Japan, and is practiced by both men and women.

The earliest otedama toys were essentially tiny drawstring bags, but they evolved into a wonderful variety of shapes — pillows, balls, fish, birds, dolls, and fruits. You can find more modern-looking otedama on many Japanese toy websites today, but we're going to go with tradition, and learn to make a simple "pillow-style" otedama — a design that originated sometime in the 15th century. Then, we'll explore some ways to make variations.

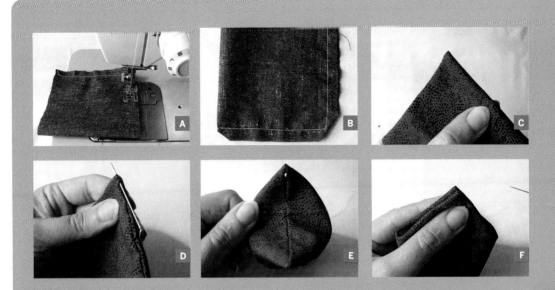

Fig. A: Using a ¼" seam allowance, sew along the 4" edge and one of the ends. Fig. B: Clip the corners, so the pillow will turn right side out more neatly. Fig. C: Poke a chopstick into the corners to make them extra sharp. Fig. D: On the seam opposite the open end, pass your needle into the seam and back out at a corner. This will hide the knot in your thread. Fig. E: Now flatten the seam so the 2 corners will stick up. (See how your knot is placed?) Fig. F: Bring the 2 corners together, and tack them with 3–5 tiny stitches.

MATERIALS

- » **4"×7¼" scrap fabric** Silk is a traditional otedama material, but quilting cottons may be easier to work with. You'll need 1 piece of scrap fabric for each otedama you make.
- » **Sewing machine** You can, of course, sew your otedama together by hand. If you do, be sure to use very small stitches, so the filling won't leak out.
- » **Scissors**
- » **Chopstick**
- » **Small sewing needle** and thread that matches your fabric
- » **Filling** Traditional fillings are adzuki beans or short-grain rice.
- » **Long quilting pin**
- » **Felt scraps and buttons (optional)** for embellishments

Diane Gilleland produces CraftyPod (craftypod.com), a blog and podcast about making stuff. She also runs DIY Alert (diyalert.com), a website devoted to crafty things in her hometown of Portland, Ore.

START »

Making the Basic Otedama

1. Fold your scrap fabric in half, right sides together, so you join the two 4" edges.

2. Adjust the stitch length on your sewing machine to 2mm. Then sew the 2 layers of fabric together along the 4" edge and one of the ends, using a ¼" seam allowance, as shown in Figure A.

NOTE: I'm using contrasting thread for visibility here; you'll want to use matching thread.

3. Clip the corners, and press the seams open with either your fingers or an iron.

4. Turn the otedama right side out, poking the corners with a chopstick so they turn out nice and sharp.

5. Locate the seam at the bottom of your otedama. This is the seam that's opposite to the open end. Thread a needle, and tie a knot in the thread. Pass the needle into this seam, and bring it back out at the corner of the otedama, as shown in Figure D. (This step will hide your knot.)

Fig. G: On your last stitch, make a knot by passing the needle through the stitch twice, and then pulling it tight. **Fig. H:** Set the otedama, open end up, on a flat surface. Fill with your favorite filling. **Fig. I:** Turn under a ¼" hem along the top edge, and pin the front and back sides together. **Fig. J:** Sew the top together with a tiny whipstitch. **Fig. K:** Bring the 2 corners together and tack. **Fig. L:** Pat the otedama into shape, and it's done.

6. Put the 2 corners together as shown in Figure F. Take 3–5 tiny stitches through both corners, tacking them together at the point where they meet. On your last stitch, leave a small loop in the thread, pass your needle through it twice, then pull it tight. This makes a secure knot (Figure G). Now your otedama has a nice, square end.

7. To fill your otedama, turn it so that the open end faces up, and set it on a flat surface (Figure H). Fill with the filling of your choice, until the filling level is about 1½" from the top edge of the fabric.

8. Turn under a ¼" hem around the top edge of the fabric. Press it in place with your fingers, and then secure the 2 sides together with a pin (Figure I).

9. Sew the end of the otedama closed using tiny whipstitches (Figure J). Knot the end of the thread as you did in Step 6.

10. Flatten this seam, and tack the remaining 2 corners together as you did in Step 6. Pat your otedama into shape, and it's finished (Figure L).

Variation: Piecework Otedama

You can create beautiful otedama by adding more fabrics. For a 2-color otedama, start with 2 pieces

of fabric, each measuring 4"×3¾". Place right sides together, and sew along 3 sides, as shown in Figure 1. Then proceed with the basic instructions.

For a 4-color otedama, start with 4 pieces of fabric, each measuring 4"×2⅛". Stitch them together in pairs. Place these 2 pieces right sides together, alternating the patterns as shown in Figure 2. Sew together on 3 sides and proceed with the basic instructions.

Variation: Otedama Fruits

Traditionally, fruit-shaped otedama were very popular in Japan, as heralds of the changing seasons.

1. To make fruit-shaped otedama, follow Step 1 of the basic instructions. Then follow Step 2, but leave 2 edges of the otedama unsewn, the top and bottom.

2. Next, with the right sides of the fabric together, take one of the open ends of the fabric, and turn a ¼" hem toward the outside. Press it in place with your fingers. Thread a needle with doubled thread, and tie a large knot in the thread.

3. Make a gathering stitch all the way around the hem, as shown in Figure 3. Pull the thread to gather the fabric as tightly as possible (Figure 4). Then

Fig. 1: A 2-color otedama starts with 2 pieces of 4"×3¾" fabric, right sides together, sewn along 3 sides. Fig. 2: A 4-color otedama starts with 4 pieces of 4"×2⅛" fabric, stitched together in pairs, then placed in alternating patterns. Fig. 3: For a fruit otedama, make a ¼" hem and run a gathering stitch through it. Fig. 4: Pull the gathering thread tight to close the bottom. Fig. 5: Filling the fruit, in this case with rice. Fig. 6: The center of the top seam is pulled down when making an owl otedama.

take a few stitches across the center opening to seal it up, so your filling won't leak out.

4. Turn the otedama right side out. Fill with the filling of your choice, stopping when the filling is 1" from the edge of the fabric.

5. Turn a ¼" hem to the inside of the remaining raw edge of fabric (Figure 5). Then, repeat Step 2 above to gather and close.

6. Sew on some felt leaves. You can even embroider some veins on the leaves for an extra touch.

Variation: Otedama Animals

Animal otedama are popular in Japan today, and they're a fun way to get kids excited about juggling. To make the owl, dog, and fish otedama shown on page 50, begin with a piece of fabric that's 4¾"×7". Follow the basic instructions through Step 9. Then, to make an owl otedama, fold the top seam down in the center. Take a few stitches to hold in place (Figure 6). Add felt and button embellishments.

To make a fish otedama, run a gathering stitch across the unfilled part, about ½" above the top of the filling. Pull the gathering stitch to make a tail. Add felt or fabric fins, and felt or button eyes.

To make a dog otedama, flatten the top of the otedama so that the 2 corners stick out to the sides. Take a few small stitches through each corner to create ears. Add felt or button embellishments.

Embellishing Your Otedama

Since otedama are made for juggling, you'll want to make sure anything you use to embellish yours is attached very securely — an otedama can take a fair amount of abuse through throwing, catching, and dropping. When I make animal otedama, I attach felt cutouts by stitching them down along every edge with a tiny whipstitch. If I add buttons, I sew them on with doubled thread, and make sure they are very secure.

You can glue embellishments on as well, but when securely sewn on they seem to stand up better to the rigors of juggling.

Learn to Juggle!

➕ Some good resources for learning to juggle:
videojug.com/film/how-to-juggle-3-balls
craftzine.com/go/juggle
craftzine.com/go/juggle3
Otedama: Traditional Japanese Juggling Toys and Games by Denichiro Onishi (Heian International, 2002)

LED HULA HOOP

Wire a hoop to put some spark in your swivel. **BY BROOKELYNN MORRIS**

Photography and illustration by Nat Wilson-Heckathorn

L ED hula hoops are so beautiful to watch, and creating a custom hoop is a satisfying challenge. Twenty-one LEDs are used in this hoop; 6 are flashing LEDs that cycle through the colors of the rainbow. Each light is combined with a resistor and then wired together in a classic and simple parallel circuit.

Be sure to research each part and its specs when creating the circuit design. Each LED for this project was chosen for its similar voltage drop, making things simpler by requiring only one value of resistor.

The battery for this project can be a laptop battery like the one used here, or a few AAA batteries taped into series. Either way, the tube can be taken apart for the battery to be easily changed. Experimentation and thoughtful research will make this project successful.

MATERIALS

» **Translucent plastic tubing, about 12'**
I used HDPE plastic, ¾" outer diameter
x 0.75 wall, "natural" color, product
#58017 from usplastic.com.

The tubing must be translucent so
that light can be emitted from within,
and HDPE's natural color is a translucent milky white. It must be stiff, yet
easy to bend in a circle. The diameter is
an important consideration: ¾" tubing
is less expensive but trickier to fit the
circuit and battery into, while 1" tubing
costs more but gives more options for
batteries and their holders. A common
package length is 100', enough for
almost 10 hoops.

» **Barbed pipe fitting** to match tubing
diameter, from the plumbing or garden
section of a hardware store
» **White electrical tape**
» **Switch** Almost any kind will do, so long
as it fits into the hoop.
» **3.6V lithium CMOS battery with
axial leads**
» **Resistors**
» **LEDs (21)** of any color, including
multicolored flashers
» **22-gauge wire** with white insulation
» **Stiff wire** like an unbent coat hanger
» **PVC pipe cutter**
» **Measuring tape**
» **Razor blade**
» **Soldering iron and solder**
» **Sponge**
» **Wire cutters**
» **Needlenose pliers**
» **Epoxy or hot glue (optional)**

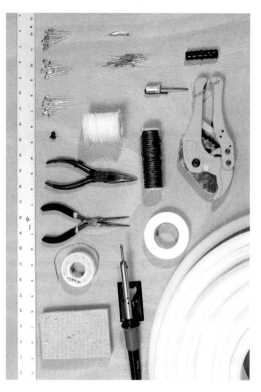

START »

1. Create the "rails" for the circuit.

a. Determine the circumference of your hoop. This
example is 126", or 10½', for a 40" diameter, same
size as a pro hoop (Wham-O's hoops are 30"–36").
Cut 2 lengths of the insulated wire at least that length
plus 1' tails to help thread the circuit into the hoop.
Mark 1 length of wire where each LED will be placed.
The 21 LEDs in this hoop were spaced every 6".

b. Mark the second wire with the same intervals, but
offset 2" from those on the first wire. After all the
marks are made on both wires, use a razor blade
to strip about ½" of insulation at each mark. The
"railroad ties" set into the "rails" will be diagonal.

This technique has advantages. When the wires
are inserted into the tube, and the rails are pressed
close together, each contact has insulated wire
against it, instead of another contact. If spaced
right, the rails are unable to short-circuit against
each other. (As insurance, cover everything with
electrical tape to prevent catastrophic shorts.)

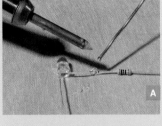

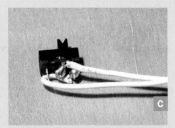

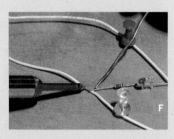

Fig. A: Solder the long end of each LED to a resistor.
Fig. B: The LEDs and resistors, soldered together in pairs.
Fig. C: The switch, with wires soldered to 2 leads.
Fig. D: Twist the LED cathodes to the negative rail and
the resistors to the positive rail. Arranging the ties on

the diagonal helps prevent shorts. Fig. E: With all the
lights attached, use the battery to test for continuity
before soldering anything. Fig. F: Use thumbtacks to
hold the rails in place while soldering all the components.

2. Solder the components.

a. With the rails complete, begin the ties. Prepare each resistor by cutting the last ⅓ off one of its lead wires (it doesn't matter which). With needle-nose pliers, curl the cut end of the lead onto itself, creating a small loop. Prepare each LED by bending the long lead — the anode (positive) — at a right angle to the base of the light. Leave the short lead — the cathode (negative) — straight. Cut the last ¼ off the end of the anode and slip it into the curled end of the resistor.

Take the pliers and curl the LED anode around the resistor, locking them together. This makes soldering easier. Now solder the place where the 2 are joined. Repeat this step until each resistor has been joined to each LED.

b. Wiring of the switch depends on the switch itself. Mine has 3 leads, but only 2 are needed to make the circuit. A 3-lead switch should be tested to see which 2 leads will make an open/closed circuit. Now add a few inches of wire to the chosen leads to make the switch accessible from inside the hoop.

3. Assemble the lights.

a. The 2 wire rails run parallel, one positive and the other negative. Wire all the components to the

rails by twisting the leads around the sections of stripped wire. Connect the LED cathodes to the negative rail and the resistors to the positive rail, placing your colored LEDs in any pattern desired.

Wire each one, and then, before soldering, press the rail wires against the battery's positive and negative terminals to check that all is in working order. If the LEDs do not light, check for loose twists and proper polarity. When each LED lights properly, smile.

b. Carefully solder each component to the rails. Wrap with electrical tape any exposed areas that could possibly short out. Now mark each end of each wire as positive or negative, for later reference. This step is very important.

4. Create and thread the hoop.

a. Cut the tubing to 10½'. If it's too tightly coiled, gently bend it, and if necessary, apply heat from hot water or a blow dryer to soften it so that it can be plied into a circle. *Very* slowly, thread the circuit into the tube. When I made this hoop, even gentle threading made one of the weaker components break, requiring a repair with electrical tape. Go slowly, and use the stiff wire to fish out the ends if there is a snag.

b. Choose one end of the tube for the switch and battery. The switch will be set at the outside edge of

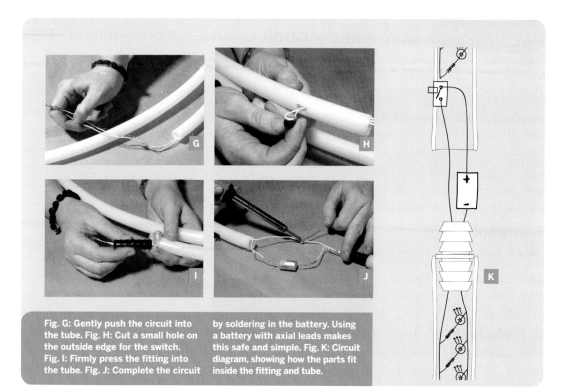

Fig. G: Gently push the circuit into the tube. Fig. H: Cut a small hole on the outside edge for the switch. Fig. I: Firmly press the fitting into the tube. Fig. J: Complete the circuit by soldering in the battery. Using a battery with axial leads makes this safe and simple. Fig. K: Circuit diagram, showing how the parts fit inside the fitting and tube.

the tube. Determine where to cut the hole, leaving room for the battery, wires, and barbed pipe fitting to be stuffed into this end of the hoop. Using a razor blade, cut a small hole to set the switch in. Start small, carving out little bits at a time to make a tight fit. Press the switch into the hole, running its wires out the open end of the tube. Secure the switch with epoxy or hot glue. On the opposite end of the tube from the switch, thread the rails through the barbed fitting, and press the fitting into the tube.

5. Connect the battery and close.

a. Wire the battery into the circuit. Solder the positive battery lead to one of the switch leads, and the negative battery lead to the negative rail that's threaded through the fitting at the other end of the tube. Solder the remaining switch lead to the positive rail to complete the circuit. Before enclosing the battery and wires, test the switch several times.

b. Push the battery and wires into the hoop. The fit is tight! Press the open end onto the barbed fitting to seal the hoop. The tube can be reopened to change the battery by gripping and pulling the ends apart. Now flip the switch and blaze up that hoop!

Brookelynn Morris is creative, and Nat Wilson-Heckathorn is a genius. Together they are creative genuises.

Soldering Is So Easy

Solder virgins, never fear! Imagine a soldering iron as a conductive-metal glue gun. A glue gun uses heat to melt glue that is sticky and liquid, and cools quickly. The soldering iron is similar: it's a heat element that melts the metal solder into small drops of hot liquid metal. Just press the tip of the iron against the wires to be soldered to heat them up for 2–3 seconds, then touch the solder right onto the connection and watch it melt, forming a liquid metal connection. Just as with a glue gun, after the melted material has been laid on, it quickly cools and hardens. Be sure to remove the iron and the solder while the drop is still hot, so they don't stick to the connection. Apply the solder like a glue gun, but then brush it like paint: make a smoothing, rubbing motion with the tip.

Don't be afraid to try this technique for the first time. The tools are available for $10, and as with anything new, practice makes perfect. Feel free to burn through a foot of solder making practice drops onto practice joined wires. It's very satisfying to watch the metal melt and to see the perfect soldered connection.

■▶ For a great video soldering tutorial, visit **craftzine.com/go/solder.**

Felt Needlebook

These handy little needlebooks are a fun present to make on the fly for a fellow crafter. The pages inside are perfect for storing sewing necessities, and the vintage button closure conceals a snap. Whip one up for yourself to take along on your next trip, or use it to bring small swatches of material to match thread or trims at the fabric store.

You will need: 8½"×11" piece of wool felt, small piece of contrasting patterned fabric, sewing machine, pinking shears, scissors, vintage button, small snap set, needle and thread, plus an assortment of sewing pins and needles to tuck inside

1. Cut out pages.

Using pinking shears, cut 2 pieces of felt, each 4"×7", leaving a small tab extending 1" extra on the short side of 1 piece (as shown), edged with scissors.

2. Embellish the cover.

Fold the 2 pieces of felt like an 8-page book, with the tabbed piece on the outside, and the tab itself on the bottom of the layers. Cut a 2½"×2" rectangle out of the print fabric, and arrange it on the front of the book so it's centered nicely. Set your sewing machine to a tight zigzag stitch and appliqué all 4 sides of the fabric square onto the front piece of felt.

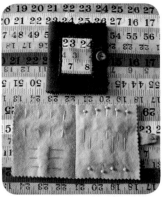

3. Bind the book.

Sew the 2 felt rectangles down the center with a straight stitch to join the pages, backstitching at the beginning and end of the seam. Now hand-sew a small snap set into place on the tab and the front of the needlebook, and embellish the tab with a vintage button.

4. Add the extras.

Fill the pages with needles, pins, and needle threaders for your next out-of-the-house sewing project!

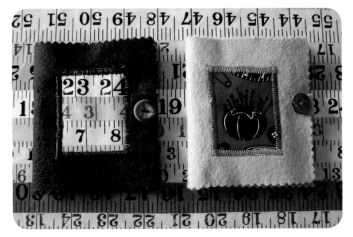

Photography by Susan Beal

Susan Beal is a Portland, Ore., writer and crafter whose new jewelry-making book, *Bead Simple*, is out in March. beadsimple.com

Craft: **PROJECTS**

Photograph by Garry McLeod

Fun is in the mix with our plush monsters, and no two are alike. Match up some fabric to make a reversible wrap skirt, and hook up electrified kerosene lanterns to make a rustic chandelier. But don't mix up your numbers when knitting math into oh-so-cute baby pants!

HAND-SEWN
FREE-RANGE
MONSTERS

By Moxie

LET YOUR CREATIVE JUICES GO WILD WITH THESE UNIQUE MIX-AND-MATCH MONSTER PLUSHES.

» My anthropomorphic creations always look like post-apocalyptic amigurumi. It's probably because I like to work free-form and I'm a little goofy on the inside.

While playing with commercial felt one day, I managed to create a hand-sewn "special friend" named Johnson. He had a comb-over and a total of six fingers, and he was glorious. In the five years since then, I've made dozens more and never the same one twice. With the nifty mix-and-match templates provided here and a deliberate rejection of precision, you can create an endless variety of special friends for you to love.

Photography by Garry McLeod; illustrations by Tim Lillis

» *The Monster at the End of This Book*, originally published in 1971, concludes with Grover learning that he has nothing to fear but fear itself.

» Kaiju Big Battel is an epic battle of egomaniacal Kaiju – villains, alien beasts, and enormous, city-crushing monsters fighting each other for world domination.

» Four artists known as Gelitin have installed a giant knitted and stuffed rabbit above the village of Artesina, in Piemonte, Italy. The rabbit took five years to knit and will remain in place until 2025.

Moxie would say "yes, please" if offered a second slice of pie. She lives with the love of her life in Seattle, and can often be found investigating spit bugs on the internet. madebymoxie.com

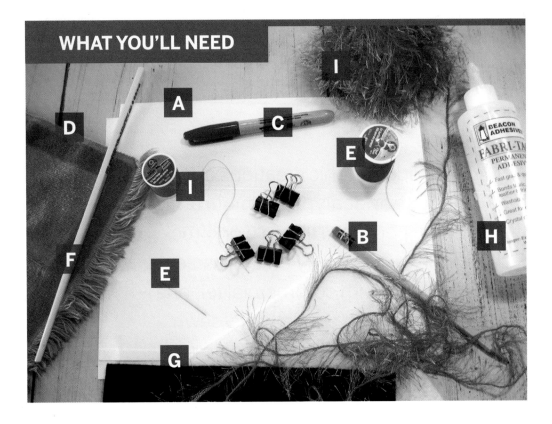

WHAT YOU'LL NEED

[A] 8½"×11" cardstock

[B] Pencil

[C] Colored marker

[D] Fabric, towel, or felt
enough for two 9"×7"
monster sides

[E] Needle and thread to
match your monster skin
or a machine that sews, if
you want to do it that way

[F] Chopstick

[G] White and black felt
1 small piece of each

[H] Fabri-Tac
or hot glue gun

[I] Fuzzy yarn and thread
to match

[NOT SHOWN]

Scissors

Poly-fil or other stuffing
like the new Nature-fil,
made of bamboo fiber
and organic cotton

1 destroyable sock

START

DESIGN AND MAKE AN ORIGINAL MONSTER

Time: 2–3 Hours Complexity: Easy

1. CREATE A FREE-RANGE MONSTER TEMPLATE

For the most part, I am an impatient, immediate-gratification crafter. I don't want to tape things before I paint them. I don't want to read the manual before I make icy beverages in the new blender, and I have no desire to measure or pin or think about anything before I sew. All the best adventures happen when you don't know where you're going. Join me, won't you?

1a. On a piece of cardstock, draw yourself a strange, roundish shape, maybe with some nubby legs and feet. Scribble away if that'd be fun, or try to draw an amoeba with your eyes closed. Add some arms that would be completely in the wrong place were this creature a real person.

1b. Loosely trace around your drawing a lot, creating tons of lines and possible shapes. Pick your favorite lines and use a marker to make one clear outline of your monster.

TIP: Keep body parts nice and fat. Any shape that's too skinny will be harder to work with later.

1c. Cut out your design, following right outside your marker line. If you have the urge to make your paper template dance around on the table, you are absolutely on the right track.

2. LAY OUT AND CUT THE MONSTER SKIN

2a. Put your monster skin on a flat surface, wrong side up.

2b. Place the template onto the fabric and trace it as accurately as you can. Use a marker or pencil that's easy to see when you cut it out, but won't bleed through to the other side. Repeat the process so you have 2 completed outlines on your fabric. If you're using patterned fabric, flip your template over before you trace it the second time. Cut out both pieces, following the outside of your lines.

3. PREP AND SEW A MONSTER CARCASS

3a. Line up the fabric pieces so you can see your drawn outlines. With the fancy monster skin, this would be called wrong side out.

3b. Optional: While I don't believe in pinning, I do like to make things easy. Using binder clips in key spots makes it easer to keep the pieces in place as you sew them together.

NOTE: Every monster needs a spot left open for turning and stuffing. Since this monster will be growing some fuzzy hair later on, we're going to leave the hole at the top of his head. That way, we can hide the seam under his delicious locks.

3c. You can use any stitch that feels good to you, or make up a new one and name it after yourself. Here's how to do a backstitch. It's easy and will make your monster seams strong and safe. Starting to the left of the designated stuffing hole, bring your needle up from the back of the carcass. Make a stitch about ¼" to the right. Bring the needle up from the back, this time about ¼" to the left of your starting place. Again, take a stitch backward. You should have 2 visible stitches right up against each other. You're backstitchin', babycakes!

Keep going, sewing all the way around the edge of the carcass, removing the clips as you go. Stop when you're about 1½" from your starting place, tie a knot, and snip off the excess thread.

3d. Trim any excess fabric from the edges of the carcass with scissors. Be careful of your stitches ... you worked hard on them.

4. TURN, STUFF, AND SEAL

4a. Put your thumbs inside the stuffing hole, and gently push the carcass sides up through the hole with your fingers. Get the bulk of the body turned before you do the limbs. Use a chopstick if you get stuck, being careful not to push through your backstitches.

4b. Fill the monster carcass with stuffing, a little at a time, starting with the limbs. Use half a handful of stuffing at a time, and use a chopstick to gently push the stuffing into place. Stop stuffing when it reaches the top of the hole.

4c. Get that threaded needle from before, throw a knot on there, and keep it close by. Fold the flaps of monster skin toward the inside of the hole. Pinch these new edges together with one hand. Grab up the needle in the other hand and sew the 2 sides together, keeping the needle on the inside flaps if you can.

4d. When the hole is almost closed, add some stuffing if you think it's needed. Push the stuffing into place, finish the seam, tie a knot, and snip! Hug your monster to celebrate.

5. ADD EYES AND A GRIN

5a. Cut a small rectangle of white felt, about 1"×2", then cut it in half. Start at a corner of one of the squares and cut out an imperfect circle. Repeat this on the other square, and stop 'cause you see the whites of his eyes! Also from the white felt, cut out 2 teeny, tiny, roundish pieces. These will be the sparkle that will bring the monster to life. Finally, using black felt cut out 2 smaller circles for the pupils.

5b. For the zig-zaggy teeth, start with another rectangle about 1"×2", cut out of green felt. Make diagonal snips along the bottom edge, creating a pleasantly uneven row of sawtooth-patterned teeth.

5c. Assemble the eyes with some Fabri-Tac between each layer, then glue them onto the monster's face. Apply glue to the back of the teeth (toothpick recommended!) and glue them down. Gently press your hand over the glued pieces to make sure they adhere.

✳ TIP: **If extra glue gets anywhere you don't want it to be, a bit of nail polish remover on a Q-tip will clean it up pretty well. Another solution is to decide not to care.**

6. COVER THE NEKKIDNESS

Depending on the size and length of your monster, you might want to give him some fancy duds. Socks are an excellent source of easy, no-sew fashion.

6a. Lay the sock down on top of the monster to make the appropriate design decisions. Cut off the extra fabric at the bottom. Cut it short for a belly shirt, or leave it long for a dress.

6b. Decide where the neckline will be and snip off the top of the sock. Cut half-circles for armholes.

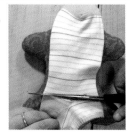

✳ **TIP:** The sock will stretch and change a bit once the monster is wearing it. Err on the side of too much sock, so that you have more cutting options once the sock is being worn.

6c. No matter what the monster says, he is simply not capable of putting his new shirt on himself. Not unlike a small child, struggle to put his outfit on him before he runs out of the house to play.

Pull the shirt on over his head, and stick his arms through the holes you made. Pull down the bottom of the shirt and shift it around until you like the way it sits. Make alterations as needed. Don't worry about fraying edges — monsters like it that way.

7. ADD SOME HAIR

Take a step back and look at your little friend. If you're chuckling to yourself and mocking him, you've got yourself a great monster. Now you can add some hair to complete his look.

7a. Using a color similar to your fuzzy yarn, thread the needle and knot the ends, same as before. Push the needle through the surface of the back of the monster's head and come back out, as if you are making a very short stitch on the underside of his scalp. Pull the thread through, but not too hard, or the scalp will pucker.

7b. Run the needle through the end of the yarn, but don't pull the thread through. About 1" down, push the needle through the yarn again, creating a loop sitting on the needle. Repeat this loop process 6 or 7 times to create a little bundle of yarn loops, all of them still hanging on the needle.

7c. Make another small behind-the-scalp stitch near your first one, holding the yarn loops against the scalp with your other hand. Pull the thread through carefully to avoid knots. Pull the thread tight enough that the yarn bundles securely against the scalp, but not so tight that the back of the monster head puckers. Continue looping the yarn and stitching the scalp. Fill in the scalp, forehead, and sideburns with hair bundles as you see fit, and watch as you create a big fuzzy head of monster hair.

7d. When you've covered his noggin in hair, tie a knot against the scalp under a patch of hair so it can't be seen, and snip the thread and yarn. Hold the monster in one hand and make him bob his head up and down really fast, like a headbanger. Watch his beautiful hair wiggle and fly in the breeze. This is a good time to make beatbox noises and make your monster dance to your rhythm.

FINISH

CARING FOR YOUR NEW MONSTER PAL

Name

If you don't give your monster a name, he will not be able to make reservations at his favorite restaurant. Good names are often ones you'd never be able to name a child. Examples: Chauncey, Smudge, Burrito.

Personality Traits

Assigning your monster a few odd quirks can paint a clear picture of who he is on the inside. Examples: Suspicious of flan. Makes audible tsk-tsks, but will not mind if you use the last of the toothpaste. Solely dedicated to the "forgotten art" of cornhusking.

Misadventures

A bored monster will be more likely to develop night terrors and bad skin. Be sure to provide a lot of open-ended and creative activities for you and monster to do together. Examples: Take your monster bowling; rent him shoes and buy him a beer. Pretend to have loud arguments with your monster while riding on the bus. Make your monster a MySpace page. Hold a highly publicized staring contest with the odds in Vegas coming in at 40:1 in favor of the monster.

 VARIATIONS ON A MONSTER

Monster Skin

You've got felt, towels you swiped from a motel, or sheets you don't sleep on anymore. I find the best and cheapest place for crazy monster skin to be the children's clothing section of my local thrift store. For a couple of bucks, you can take home a bright pink fun-fur jacket or a pair of bright blue corduroy pants. Cut the clothes up, making sure to maximize the usable flat parts of the fabric.

⚠ **WARNING: While children's clothing at the thrift store comes in an unlimited number of colors and textures, it too often comes fully equipped with the undesirable smells of sour milk and feet. Wash your monster skin treasures first, so your monster starts life fresh and clean.**

Body Image

Get started with our simple designs for body shapes, limbs, and eyes and teeth (shown here), all downloadable as PDFs from craftzine.com/06/ monsters. Then mix and match, cut and paste, and generally throw together the different pieces to create an endless variety of monsters.

❈ **TIP: Bodies, eyes, and teeth can be used at any angle. Try making a long, horizontal monster, or a monster with a tiny head and huge bottom.**

Hairiness

Using your yarn of choice, vary the length of the loops to create different hairdos. Examples: Short loops in the front with longer loops in the back gets you a monster mullet. Short loops in a row around the back from temple to temple will make a semi-bald monster — add a bit of velcro and faux fur and you've got a monster toupée. How about yarn bundles under each arm for some armpit fluff?

THAT'S A WRAP!

By Andrea DeHart

TAKE TWO COMPLEMENTARY FABRICS AND SEW THEM INTO ONE WRAPAROUND, REVERSIBLE SKIRT.

▶▶ The 70s had their fair share of fashion statements, including platform shoes, bell-bottoms, and caftans, to name a few. One of the more creative fashions that became popular was the infamous wrap skirt. It gave women all the style and comfort of an A-line skirt, with the added ability to expand and contract to fit our ever-changing waistlines. Although the general pattern stays the same, this modern variation is reversible with a scoop pocket and bold ribbon waistband.

If you're new to sewing, this is a perfect project. The pattern is simple and quick to complete. There are no fasteners, hems, or waistband panels to worry about. For the pros, there's a fancy advanced version with buttons and elastic instead of ribbon ties.

» Skirts are the second-oldest garments known to humankind, predated only by loincloths.

» It's a popular myth in the United States that shorter skirt hems mean booming financial times and longer hemlines mean bad news for the stock market.

» In the early 60s, British fashion designer Mary Quant was one of the many designers who is credited for inventing the mini-skirt, naming it after her favorite car, the Mini.

Andrea DeHart, aka CraftyBitch (**craftybitch.com**), is the creator of handmade handbags, wallets, doggie couture, and most recently, a little girl.

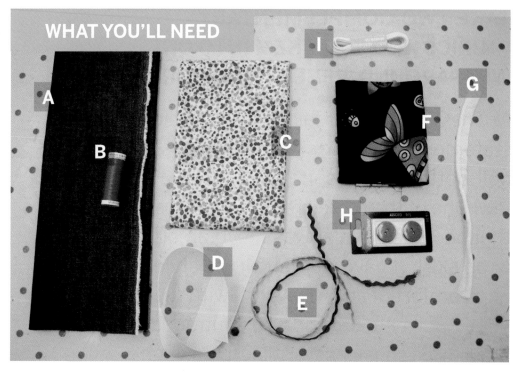

WHAT YOU'LL NEED

[A] 2yds 45" (or 1½yds 60") solid denim, twill, or canvas fabric light to medium weight

[B] Spool of contrasting thread

FOR BEGINNER PATTERN:
[C] 2yds 45" (or 1½yds 60") patterned cotton fabric lightweight

[D] 3yds 1½" grosgrain ribbon

[E] ¼yd rickrack or decorative trim for pocket

FOR ADVANCED PATTERN:
[F] 2½yds 45" (or 2yds 60") patterned cotton fabric lightweight

[G] 4yds of ½" wide piping

[H] Large buttons (2)

[I] Cord elastic 6½"

[NOT SHOWN]

Usual sewing supplies

An iron

BEGINNER

ADVANCED

Photography by Sam Murphy (top) and Jen Siska (bottom)

▶ A CONVERTIBLE WRAP SKIRT DOUBLES YOUR CREATIVITY

Beginner Pattern Time: **2–4 hours** Complexity: **Easy**
Advanced Pattern Time: **4–6 hours** Complexity: **Medium**

1. CHOOSE YOUR FABRIC

Your first step is fabric selection. Keep in mind that you'll see a peekaboo of the second fabric from time to time, so you may want to find 2 fabrics that complement each other. Select a patterned fabric that's lightweight, preferably a woven cotton. An overall random print works best and doesn't require any additional yardage for aligning stripes or plaids. For the solid fabric, look for a light- to medium-weight denim, twill, or canvas. Thicker fabrics are much more difficult to sew and don't drape as nicely. Avoid stretch knits or sheer fabrics (no one needs to see all your seams).

NOTE: Don't forget to pre-wash your fabrics, including your ribbon trim, before you make that first cut. You only have to make this mistake once and then you'll never do it again.

2. CUT OUT THE PATTERN PIECES

Download and print the pattern from craftzine.com/06/wrapskirt. The pattern was sized for a 30" waist, just below the navel. To enlarge or reduce to fit your measurements, follow the guidelines on the pattern pieces. The finished length of the skirt is 25", but can also be adjusted as necessary. Pin the pattern pieces to the fabric, aligning the grain line on the pattern to match the grain line of your fabrics.

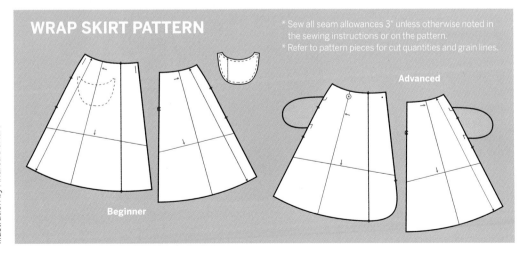

WRAP SKIRT PATTERN

* Sew all seam allowances 3" unless otherwise noted in the sewing instructions or on the pattern.
* Refer to pattern pieces for cut quantities and grain lines.

Beginner

Advanced

Illustration by Andrea DeHart

3. SEW THE SOLID FABRIC SKIRT PANELS

3a. The solid fabric side of the skirt is very straightforward so it's best to start here. Stay-stitch the front and back waistline edges to prevent stretching. Start from the center and sew toward the outside edges approximately ½" from the edge.

3b. With right sides together, join the center back seam of the back skirt sections, matching the pattern symbols for placement. Sew each front skirt panel to the back skirt panels at the side seams. With an iron, press all seams open to lie flat.

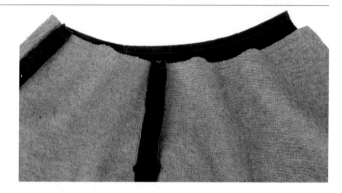

Advanced Pattern:

3c. Pin piping ⅝" from the edges around the entire skirt, except for the waistband side. Sew as close to the piping as your machine allows. Clip the seams around the curves to eliminate bulk.

To add the elastic band for closure, measure down 1" on the center front panels at the waistline and mark with a pin. Cut 2 strips of cord elastic 3¼" long, and fold them in half. Position each at the 1" mark on either side of the opening with the loop facing away from the raw edge. Using a very small stitch, sew the elastic cord along the piping seam line. Reinforce stitches to prevent the cord from slipping out.

Photography by Andrea DeHart

4. SEW THE PATTERNED FABRIC SKIRT PANELS

4a. Stay-stitch the waistband edges and join the back center seam as described in Step 3.

Beginner Pattern:

4b. Don't hesitate to adjust the pocket shape to suit your level of sewing. For example, square patch pockets are much easier to sew than rounded edge shapes. The key to the pockets is to avoid too much bulk, as this may add inches to your hips when worn with the reverse side facing outward. To make the patch pocket, press under a ⅜" seam allowance around all sides. Sew rickrack trim to the top of the pocket as shown.

4c. Pin the pocket to the outside side of the skirt, matching the pattern symbols for placement, and topstitch in place. Sew each front skirt panel to the back skirt panels at the side seams. With an iron, press all seams open to lie flat.

Advanced Pattern:

4b. To make the hip slit pockets, sew the front and back skirt panels along the sides with right sides together. Reinforce stitching at the corners of the pockets, and clip up to these corners. Press open the side seams and trim 1 layer of the pocket lining.

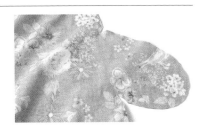

4c. On the wrong side of the fabric, pin the pocket lining toward the center front of the skirt. Stitch through all layers, following the original pocket lining seam as your guide.

5. COMBINE THE 2 SKIRTS

Lay the solid skirt out on a large, flat surface with the right side facing you. With right sides together, lay the patterned skirt face down, matching all edges, and pin.

Beginner Pattern:

5a. Sew the 2 skirts together along the side seams and bottom edge, keeping the waistband side open.

5b. Clip the seams along the corners and the skirt hemline.

5c. Turn the skirt with right sides facing out and press all the edge seams flat. Topstitch ¼" from the edge with a contrasting thread.

Advanced Pattern:

5a. A trick to sewing piping is to follow the original stitch line that was used to attach the piping. In this case, sew with the solid fabric panel facing toward you.

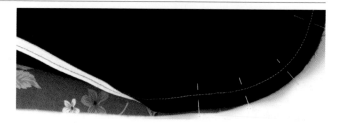

5b. Sew around all the edges, including the waistband, leaving a 6" opening along the hemline at the center back. Clip all the corners and trim approximately ¼" around the edge of the solid fabric to reduce bulk. Turn your fabric right side out through the back hem opening and hand-stitch closed, using an invisible stitch.

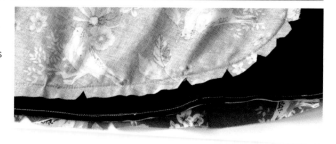

6. FINISH THE WAISTBAND

Beginner Pattern:

6a. Using a long stitch, baste along the waistband edge to close the opening and keep the panels from shifting. To calculate the length of the waistband ribbon, measure the total length of the waistband, adding an extra 18" on each side for the ties (72" total for a 30" waist). Align the center of the ribbon with the center back of the waistband. Pin ¾" from the edge and baste in place.

✻ **TIP: To align the ribbon correctly, first fold it in half lengthwise and gently press with an iron. The crease will work as a guideline when positioning the ribbon.**

6b. Wrap the excess ribbon around to the opposite side of the skirt and pin in place. Stitch along the edge of the ribbon, going through all thicknesses. Use a straight stitch, zigzag stitch, or any other decorative stitch that you like. Remove the basting stitch once the waistband ribbon is secure.

6c. For the side ties, cut two 18" lengths of ribbon. With the patterned side of the skirt facing outward, sew 1 tie to the left hip along the waistband. Repeat with the solid side. The ties will be on the opposite hips, as shown at far right. Finish the ends of the ribbon with a narrow hem.

Advanced Pattern:

Topstitch the waistband edge for reinforcement. Now try on the skirt and mark where the buttons should go. Sew one button on the patterned side, the other on the opposite side of the solid fabric. Or you can add multiple buttons along the waistband for a more decorative (and more functional) look.

7. WRAP YOURSELF UP

Wrap skirts come in 2 styles — flap in the front and flap in the back. I prefer my flaps in the front — if a gust of wind blows your skirt, it's a lot easier to control the front flap. But the back flap allows for front pocket details and a smoother silhouette in front. It's your call.

Beginner Pattern:

Tie the left ribbon with the right inner hip ribbon. Make a secure knot that lies nicely under your skirt panel and can easily untie when needed. Cross the right panel over the left. Tie the 2 remaining ribbons together (knot or bow). When the skirt is reversed, you should be able to repeat the sequence exactly.

Advanced Pattern:

Repeat the steps above, but substitute the elastic loops and buttons for the ties.

FINISH

CAMP LAMP
CHANDELIER

By Matt Maranian

HANG KEROSENE LANTERNS ON STURDY BRANCHES FOR A RUSTIC TWIST ON HOME LIGHTING.

▶▶ Bring the great outdoors in and experience the romance of roughing it under the stars without the threat of a kerosene-fueled conflagration!

The juxtaposition of the craggy birch branches and banged-up kerosene lanterns works well with the self-consciously minimal hardware. I passed on the ubiquitous swag chain, instead opting for an exposed cord attached to a fine cable, which reeks of sleek contemporary Italian design — and what better thing to reek of?

Although the chandelier is designed to hang from a hard-wired ceiling junction box, the design would be perfectly viable as a swag too, should you be short on ceiling junction boxes.

» The ornate chandelier at Graceland, Elvis' home in Memphis, features over 80 hand-cut crystals and weighs more than 600 pounds.

» At a French opera house in 1906, large pieces of the chandelier fell and crashed onto the audience. It is said to be the inspiration for the Gaston Leroux novel and later, more famously, the Broadway musical, *The Phantom of the Opera*.

» The earliest chandeliers were used in medieval churches and abbeys to light large areas. They were simple in form, made of wood, and illumined by candles.

Photography by Matt Maranian; illustrations by Tim Lillis

Matt Maranian is a designer and best-selling author who lives in Brattleboro, Vt. A revised, updated edition of his cult classic, *L.A. Bizarro* (Chronicle Books), is scheduled for release in spring of 2009.

WHAT YOU'LL NEED

[A] Kerosene lanterns (3) ideally of varying size and color

[B] Medium-sized wire nuts (2)

[C] Small tube of metal-to-metal epoxy

[D] 6' lamp cord, plus the length at which you want the chandelier to hang i.e. the "ceiling extension"

[E] Medium-grade sandpaper

[F] 40-watt ceiling fan bulbs (3)

[G] ¼"×4" eye bolt and acorn nut (or longer, if necessary)

[H] ¹⁄₁₆" cable ferrules (2)

[I] ¹⁄₁₆" aircraft cable cut to the length at which you want the chandelier to hang

[J] 1"×¹⁄₈ IP brass washers (3)

[K] 2"×¹⁄₈ IP threaded steel nipples (3)

[L] 2" keyless chandelier sockets (3)

[M] Spring clamps (optional) 2 or more

[NOT SHOWN]

Strong branches (2) plus smaller extras for final decoration

Newspaper

4" zip ties

Long twist ties (3)

Sand, salt, or fine gravel if needed

Chalk or marker or anything that will show when used on the branch bark

Phillips head screwdriver to loosen terminal screws on light sockets

Scissors

Pliers

Handsaw

Gardening shears

Drill with ¼" bit

Glue gun

⏩ WIRE OLD CAMP LANTERNS TO MAKE A RUSTIC CHANDELIER

Time: 4–6 Hours Complexity: Medium

1. SELECT BRANCHES AND LANTERNS

1a. Choose branches with a circumference of at least 5" (but not much more), preferably dry (dead), and most definitely free of rot. The branches used here were each about 24" in length and were selected for their arch, branch variation, fungal decoration, and node accents. Avoid pine if possible, as it will gum up your drill bit and drip tar over time.

1b. Old-time kerosene lanterns are plentiful secondhand; old guys selling tools and camping stuff at flea markets tend to have them, and the classic American roadside junk barn is always a safe bet. Choose lanterns that look the most road-weary and rusted, and make sure they're completely bone-dry of all kerosene. The glass globes featuring a layer of sooty black crust are the most desirable for this application; if you have trouble finding one, make like a prop master and lightly spritz the inside of the glass with black spray paint, then scrape some of the paint away with some steel wool or fine sandpaper for convincingly faux filth.

2. CONSTRUCT THE FORM

2a. Cut the ends of the branches to your desired length with a handsaw. Cut ends on an angle or with a faceted cut. Clean up nodes and small branches if necessary by trimming with a pair of gardening shears, also at an angle. Smooth cut ends with a light sanding.

2b. The framework of the chandelier is more or less an X made of 2 branches. Determine which branch is to be the lower half of the X and which is to be the top half. To find their point of balance, center the bottom branch on the very tip of the corner of your worktable, adjusting for balance.

Next, center the top branch over the balanced lower branch, forming the X, so that the 2 balance with each other on the same point. This may take some minor adjustments before you find their combined axis.

2c. Once you determine the axis, mark that spot on the top branch, remove the branch, and mark the corresponding axis spot on the bottom branch. Drill the axis through both branches.

2d. Reposition the branches as they were when balanced, and slide the eye bolt through the drilled axis leads, so that the eye of the bolt sits on the top branch. Attach the acorn nut at the end of the bolt and gently tighten.

3. ELECTRIFY THE LANTERNS

3a. Remove the glass globe from the lantern by pulling the spring-loaded top up and away from the glass, while simultaneously lowering the side lever on the lantern. If the lantern has a wick in place, remove it. Unscrew the cap on the kerosene tank, and yank off the attached stop chain.

3b. Leaving the globe cage in its release position, secure the lantern upside down. Spring clamps work well for this, but any means by which you can secure the lantern will suffice.

3c. Slide the cardboard casing off the chandelier socket. Screw the threaded nipple into its base, as far as the socket will allow, but don't tighten. Screw a threaded washer onto the end of the nipple, but only far enough to be flush with its end. Screw in the bulb.

3d. Roll a piece of newspaper into a loose, narrow tube, and cut to about 8" in length.

3e. Mix the epoxy as per product instructions, and spread generously over the bottom end of the washer and threaded nipple. Center the socket assembly into the upturned lantern top, and nestle the crumpled newspaper around the bulb to keep the socket assembly stationary while the epoxy sets.

3f. Once the epoxy has dried to full strength, remove the newspaper and unscrew the socket from the threaded nipple.

3g. Cut a piece of lamp cord to 2' in length. With a pair of scissors, make a 1" snip down its center at one end, and pull the 2 separated wires apart, about 3". Cut around the end of each wire, only deep enough to slice through the insulation, and slide the insulation off to expose 1" of the stranded copper wire. Twist each wire individually, to keep its strands from fraying.

3h. Loosen both terminal screws on the light socket. Curl the twisted end of one of the cord wires around a terminal screw, and tighten into place. Repeat with the remaining cord wire on the opposite terminal screw. Slip the cardboard sleeve back over the socket.

3i. Snugly screw the wired socket back onto the threaded nipple, and draw the cord through one of the top vents of the lantern. Screw in the light bulb.

3j. Pull the spring-loaded lantern top as high as possible, and fit the glass globe over the bulb and back into its wire cage, raising the side lever back to its original upright position. Repeat Step 3 to electrify the remaining 2 lanterns.

4. PLACE THE LANTERNS

4a. Establish a place (such as a rafter in a garage) to temporarily hang the branch construction to determine the balance of the lantern placement. While holding the branch construction steady, carefully place the lanterns more or less where you'd like them, creating a general balance between the 3 points of weight.

Mark the spots at which the lanterns are placed on the top of the branch, remove the lanterns, and bring the branch construction back to your worktable.

4b. Working with one lantern at a time, re-establish the placement of the lantern handle using the hanging point marked at the top of the branch. Securely twist-tie the lamp cord next to the spot at which the handle rests on the branch, allowing enough slack in the cord so that the lantern can hang freely. Repeat with the remaining 2 lanterns.

4c. Beginning from the twist tie point, run a thin line of hot glue along the top center of the branch, working in 3" sections, to secure the cord flat against the branch. Continue to the center of the branch assembly, stopping about 2" short of the eye bolt.

5. FINAL WIRING

5a. Trim the lamp cord near the eye bolt, allowing about 4" of extra length beyond the end of the glued area. Split and expose the copper wires, as in Step 3g. Repeat with the remaining 2 lanterns.

5b. To complete the electrical connection, take only 1 exposed wire from each of the 3 lamp cords and twist them together. Take the remaining 3 exposed wires from the cords and twist those together.

5c. Cut, split, and expose the ends of the additional ("ceiling extension") lamp cord, as in Step 3g. Twist one wire of the extension cord to one twisted cluster on the chandelier, and twist the other wire to the other twisted cluster. Cap each twisted cluster by screwing on a wire nut.

6. HANG THE CHANDELIER

6a. Return the chandelier to the spot where you first hung it to balance the lanterns. If it's necessary to adjust the balance, create a ballast by adding sand, salt, or fine gravel to the kerosene tank of whichever lantern needs weight (use a funnel made from a rolled sheet of paper).

6b. Slide a ferrule down about 5" over the end of the aircraft cable. Loop the cable through the eye bolt, and bring the end back through the ferrule. Adjust the cable and the ferrule by sliding the ferrule toward the eye bolt to create the smallest and tightest loop possible, then crush the ferrule with pliers to secure. Repeat at the opposite end of the cable, to accommodate your ceiling hardware.

6c. Allowing the lamp cord a bit of slack, zip-tie the lamp cord to the cable at a point about 8" from the eye bolt. Continue to zip-tie the rest of the cord, at points spaced about 10" along the length of the cable. Cut and expose the cord's end as in Step 3g, for hard wiring.

FINISH X

EXPERIMENTS: OCTAGON = PANTS

Experiment 1. Copy Figure A and cut out the octagon. Tape the identified sides together (the sides that are supposed to be sewn), matching direction arrows as shown. First attach the sides labeled "a" together, then the "b" sides together. Notice that the result has 3 holes. One hole is formed by 2 of the original octagon sides coming together for the waist, and the other 2 holes are each formed by 1 side curling around to make a leg hole. With imagination, these are pants.

A little paper-folding helps to visualize this octagon folded in half as pants. Fold the octagon's center point a bit more than halfway up to the waist (Figure B1), and crease the middle third of this fold horizontally. (Each blue arrow in Figure B indicates an action transforming one picture to the next.) Then fold the legs down from the center of the octagon (Figure B2). This causes the sides of the paper to bend up — don't worry, allow this to happen. Let the points of the waist edges meet in the center, then crease what would be the upper thighs if these really were pants, as Figure B3 shows. Now look at the shape of the pants (Figure B4).

Those of you who have been tenaciously shopping at world clothing stores located in college towns will recognize this style, sold as Thai fisherman pants. However, even those pants don't have *such* a gathering of material at the crotch (where the inside seams of regular pants meet). We would rather have a result more like Thai wrap pants, which are loose but have no excess crotch fabric.

Topologically (in terms of the number of holes), we have successfully created pants. However, geometrically (that is, in terms of proportions, curviness, and distances), we have more work to do. Our model shows that the problem is not the sizing but the flatness of the original octagon. To avoid flatness, we'll work with curved surfaces. Positive constant curvature yields a sphere, and negative constant curvature yields a hyperbolic plane or pseudosphere; we'll approximate negative constant curvature here with paper.

Our paper approximation will consist of a set of triangles glued together. While each piece is flat, the object made from them won't be. Mathematicians say that such a surface is locally flat, but globally curved. The global curvature will come from a change in the angles around certain points in the surface; ordinarily, adding the angles around a point in a piece of paper gives 360°, but in the next 2 experiments this won't be the case.

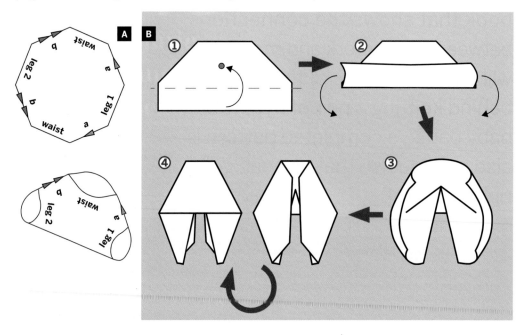

Experiment 2. Figure C shows 8 triangles that can be made into an octagon with positive average curvature unit comparable to that of a sphere. First, duplicate Figure C and cut out the shape. Crease along the edges between the triangles, then tape the arrowed sides together. Now, just as in Experiment 1, attach the *a* sides together and attach the *b* sides together. As before, the result has 3 holes, corresponding to the waist and ankles of a pair of pants. You can make the resulting shape look more pants-like by following the same folding sequence as given in Figure B2. At this point, you'll notice that material has been added in exactly the wrong region of the pants — there's even more material at the crotch!

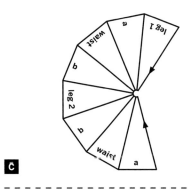

C

Experiment 3. Figure D shows 4 pairs of triangles that can be made into an octagon with negative average curvature. First, duplicate the figure and cut out the 4 shapes. Tape the arrowed sides together. Now, just as in Experiment 1, attach the *a* sides together and attach the *b* sides together. As before, the result has 3 holes, corresponding to the waist and ankles of a pair of pants. But, unlike the previous 2 experiments, this actually looks like a pair of pants!

In reality, pants designers don't use uniform curvature when making patterns. (This is why commercially available patterns don't use octagons.) They want zero curvature along the legs of the pants and zero curvature near the waist — but negative curvature near the crotch.

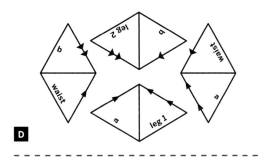

D

Knitting Pattern Construction for Hyperbolic Pants

As earlier said, a uniformly curved pair of pants can be made from an octagon. Figure E shows the usual identifications for pants, made on a flat octagon. To make pants with uniform negative curvature, we need to use a patch from a hyperbolic plane. Figure F shows a hyperbolic plane patch with pants identifications.

There are some mathematical and knitting-design aspects to the diagram that are worth noting, though most are beyond the scope of this article. The double-headed arrow marks the waist-to-waist measurement, the same length as the outseam. The inseam lies along a geodesic (the shortest line between two points) that runs through the center of the waist-to-waist to the center of

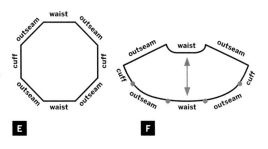

E   F

a cuff. Thus, hyperbolic pants are determined by the waist, outseam, cuff, and waist-to-waist measurements rather than by the standard waist, inseam, and cuff measurements of sewn pants. The 2 straight outseams and the waist-to-waist are measured in rows, while the other outseams, cuffs, and waist are measured in stitches.

Seamstresses reading this are now worried: most humans have much longer outseams than waist-to-waist measurements. For example, a Misses size 10 has a waist-to-waist of about 23" and an outseam of about 42". However, young children have waist-to-waist measurements that are comparable to their outseams. This allows us to use a simple design for baby-sized pants. So let's get to it!

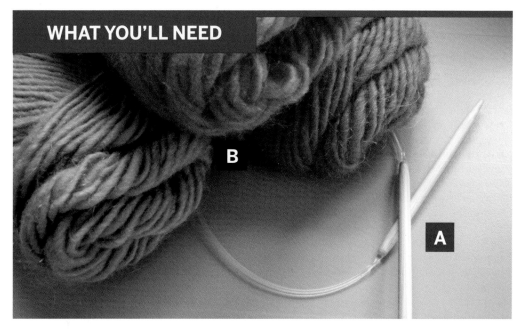

WHAT YOU'LL NEED

[A] Circular needles size 6

[B] Yarn, worsted-weight, machine-washable (300m/330yds)

[NOT SHOWN]

Thin elastic (optional)

Tapestry needle

Gauge of 5 stitches per inch and 6.5 rows per inch
In this pattern, the row gauge is as important as the stitch gauge. Possible yarns include Cascade 220 Superwash and Cascade Bollicine Maxi.

MAKING **MATHEMATICS** WITH **NEEDLEWORK**

SARAH-MARIE BELCASTRO
CAROLYN YACKEL

▶▶ This project is an edited excerpt from *Making Mathematics with Needlework* (AK Peters, Ltd.), edited by Sarah-Marie Belcastro and Carolyn Yackel. Beautifully illustrated, with complete patterns and the mathematics behind each project, the book successfully connects the worlds of mathematics and fiber arts. Each chapter contains a different mathematical paper and corresponding needlework project, from a quilted Möbius band, to the graph theory of blackwork embroidery, to hyperbolic baby pants.

The project sections are written for crafters, so that non-mathematician readers can have a tangible experience with mathematical concepts. This project has been condensed from the original chapter, so be sure to check out the book for more in-depth explanations of the mathematics!

Photography by sarah-marie belcastro (bottom and following pages) and Arwen O'Reilly (top)

▶▶ KNIT HYPERBOLIC PANTS

Time: A Weekend Complexity: Easy

A few notes on the pattern and instructions:

» This pattern is not scalable, and it is highly dependent on the gauge for fit.

» It is forgiving of small mistakes. That is, if you occasionally K40 before a decrease rather than K41, it won't matter. Just be careful near the bind-off row to make sure you have the desired number of stitches.

» Where K2tog or P2tog is marked, feel free to do whatever decrease you find quickest and easiest; it doesn't matter in terms of the finished product. Knitting/purling into the fronts/backs of the loops is fine.

» This pattern is for 6-month-old baby pants, but *Making Mathematics with Needlework* has a range of pattern sizes.

1. CAST ON

Using a long-tail cast-on, cast on 280 stitches. Place split stitch markers on the cast-on edge (not the needle) between the 45th and 46th stitches, 118th (= 45 + 73) and 119th stitches, 162nd (= 45 + 73 + 44) and 163rd stitches, and 234th (= 45 + 73 + 44 + 72) and 235th stitches. These will be used as guides for seaming the pants, and must be placed before any more knitting occurs to avoid difficulty in counting once decreases have been made.

2. KNIT THE ROWS

Row 1: *P39, P2tog*
Finish the row when the stitches run out.
Row 2: *K39, K2tog*
Finish the row when the stitches run out.
Row 3: P34, *P2tog, P39*
Finish the row when the stitches run out.
Row 4: K34, *K2tog, K39*
Finish the row when the stitches run out. Repeat this pattern 23 times, for a total of 92 rows (or until there are 44 stitches on the needles).
Row 93: Purl across. Bind off loosely purlwise.

NOTE: At this point your pants will not look like pants, but instead like a piece of a pseudosphere, as shown here.

3. SEW THE OUTSEAMS

3a. With the knitting right-side out, match the middle 2 stitch markers (on the cast-on edge) with the 2 ends of the bind-off edge.

Use an invisible vertical-to-horizontal graft to seam the cast-on edge to each selvedge. These seams begin at the waist, where the bind-off and cast-on stitches are matched, and end at the cuffs, where the remaining stitch markers meet the corner of the selvedge and cast-on edge.

3b. Every 3 or 4 stitches, graft to 2 rows instead of 1.

3c. Thread 18" of thin elastic or two 35" lengths of yarn through every other stitch just below the cast-off edge. Sew the ends of the elastic together, or tie the lengths of yarn into a bow.

FINISH ✕

Curio Case

Build a glass table that will turn knickknacks into exotic relics. BY MATT MARANIAN

I've always been a sucker for those big ol' dusty glass cases found in natural history museums or underfunded historical attractions. It never really matters what these cases actually house: a taxidermied armadillo, Abe Lincoln's top hat, the world's longest tapeworm — put almost anything in a case behind glass and it suddenly seems valuable and exotic.

To make a dusty glass case of your own that serves double duty as an intriguing side table, start with a scavenged window and some furniture legs salvaged from a thrift-shop castoff. A few dollars' worth of cheap building materials and a little paint will finish the job. Suddenly your own collection of worthless relics will have museum-quality legitimacy.

Photography by Matt Maranian

Fig. A: Sand all the edges to keep the sides of the case flush, and clear of splinters. Fig. B: A little wood glue goes a long way; apply sparingly.

Fig. C: Drill the screws flush with the surface of the wood and no deeper, or you'll risk cracking. Fig. D: Paint the top of the case bottom to show off your curios.

Materials

- » **Window**
- » **Pine boards 1"×4"×6' (2 or more)** depending on the perimeter measurement of the window
- » **Medium-grade sandpaper**
- » **Miter box**
- » **¾" MDF board 2'×4'**
- » **Circular saw or table saw** or a friend with one
- » **Wood glue**
- » **Pencil**
- » **9⁄64" drill bit**
- » **2" drywall screws (20 or so)**
- » **Paint and paintbrush/roller (optional)**
- » **2" narrow utility hinges (2)**
- » **Furniture legs and mounting plates, plus ½" screws** at the appropriate gauge for the mounting plates

1. Scavenge for materials.

First you'll need to hunt for a good window with its wood framing (sash) intact. There are 3 things to consider when scavenging or hitting an architectural salvage yard:

• The window frame needs only 1 "good" side, so you can be slightly forgiving in your selection.

• The side that faces down should have at least 1 frame member that's a minimum 2" wide to support the width of the hinges.

• Look for a frame no larger than 2'×4'. The reason for this is that the bottom of the curio case is made from MDF (medium density fiberboard), which is sold in precut 2'×4' sheets. The size of your window will, obviously, determine the size of your curio case, and a case sized larger than 2'×4' will require cutting from a 4'×8' sheet of MDF or plywood, adding cost to your project.

Next, comb a couple of thrift shops for a complete set of furniture legs, at a length of your choosing. Often you can find some crappy little table with removable legs for much less than you'd pay for a new set of legs with the mounting hardware. You're also likely to get a set of legs with a little more flair than the big-box hardware store variety.

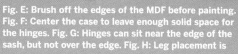

Fig. E: Brush off the edges of the MDF before painting. Fig. F: Center the case to leave enough solid space for the hinges. Fig. G: Hinges can sit near the edge of the sash, but not over the edge. Fig. H: Leg placement is arbitrary, but if the legs extend at an angle, then 2" from the edge of the case is good. Fig. I: Rotate your curios frequently. You'll be amazed how important they look when placed behind glass!

2. Build the case.

Establish which side of the window you want to be the tabletop. Now flip it over, top side down. Measure and cut the 1"×4" pine boards to create a framework of 4 sides that meet the wooden sash of the window, sitting just outside the edge of the glass. It's best to use a miter box for straight cuts, or if you're real fancy, a table saw. Sand the edges clear of splinters.

Set this framework on top of the MDF sheet to determine the size of the case bottom, by tracing the framework's perimeter. Cut the MDF to size (Figure A).

With the framework in place on the MDF board, glue the sides by dabbing some wood glue inside the edges of the end pieces. Place together and let dry (Figure B).

Drill leads for the screws at a spot ½" from each corner edge, and no more than 1" deep — it's best to tape off the drill bit to serve as a guide. Screw the sides of the case together with drywall screws (Figure C). Paint the inside and outside of the casing framework, or not.

Paint the top of the case bottom (Figure D). Once dry, place it facedown on top of the case framework, and secure with drywall screws. Space the screws by marking spots about 5" apart across each edge of the MDF, and drill leads. Once secured, paint the visible side edges of the MDF board (Figure E).

3. Final assembly.

Place the window top side down, and center the case on top of it, bottom side up (Figure F). Place the hinges 3" from the corners of the case, and mark their screw holes with a pencil (Figure G). Drill very short leads (no more than half the length of the screws), and screw the hinges into place.

Position the leg mounting plates about 2" from the edges of each corner of the case (Figure H). Mark the screw holes with a pencil, and secure into place with ½" screws. Attach the legs to the mounting plates.

4. Curate.

Flip the construction over, and fill it with your personal collections of provocative junk (Figure I). Little strips of index cards typewritten with expository info would be an excellent touch.

Matt Maranian is a designer and best-selling author who lives in Brattleboro, Vt.

Foldschool

Make a sturdy yet stylish kid-sized chair out of cardboard. BY ANNA DILEMNA

If you want a chic, affordable kid's chair that doesn't look like it's from a catalog, try Foldschooling it. This chair is unique, stylish, and totally made of cardboard! Where can you buy it? You can't. Foldschool furniture is a 100% DIY concept and therefore available only to crafters. This tutorial elaborates on the basic manual from the Foldschool site (foldschool.com). There you'll find helpful tips as well as some great suggestions on how you can pimp your chair once you've finished building it. Even if you don't have kids of your own, Foldschool chairs make fabulous gifts for small-sized friends and family.

Photography by Alejandro Jaimes

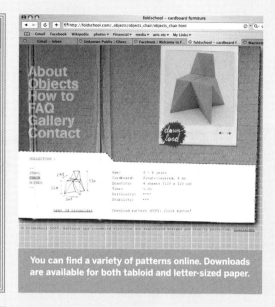

You can find a variety of patterns online. Downloads are available for both tabloid and letter-sized paper.

FINDING CARDBOARD

 You may have to be a bit resourceful in finding cardboard large enough for this project.

If you don't have a refrigerator or other large appliance box stored in your garage, check out your local large appliance stores, furniture stores, or framing shops. Some branches of paper supply stores such as Xpedx carry corrugated sheets (sometimes called "corrugated pads") of cardboard. Shipping and packaging companies are also a good bet, and although they usually sell in bulk, if you show up and beg, they may be willing to hand over the small amount that you need. Or you can buy the minimum number of sheets in bulk and have a chair-making party with friends!

It may be easier to find the cardboard in smaller pieces, in which case you should print up the patterns first so that you'll know exactly the sizes you need. (Make sure the arrows on the patterns are parallel to the direction of the lines in the cardboard!)

1. Make your pattern.

a. Download and then print the chair pattern from foldschool.com. Check the scale that's printed on the pattern to make sure you have the correct size. You can also download patterns for a stool or a rocker, and the instructions here can be applied to these items as well.

b. Cut along the faded gray lines surrounding each printed page.

c. Tape patterns together by matching the letters.

d. If you're short on cardboard, you may want to cut patterns out along the solid black lines so you can place your pieces closer together. You should have 7 pattern pieces.

2. Cut your board.

a. Place your pattern pieces onto the cardboard so that the arrows on the pattern are parallel to the lines in your board caused by the corrugations. This is important.

b. Apply spray adhesive to the wrong side of the patterns and place them on the cardboard.

c. With your cutting mat underneath, use your blade to cut the cardboard around the pattern (Figure A). Don't remove the paper pattern yet!

3. Fold and glue individual shapes.

a. Use your ruler to press creases into the cardboard along the dashed lines of the pattern. Be firm, but not so firm that you rip into the paper or board!

b. Using your needle, punch holes in the crosshatches. Make sure they pierce all the way through the board.

c. Remove the paper pattern from the cardboard.

d. Fold the cardboard upward at all the creases.

e. Apply glue to the tabs and connect them together in ascending order (first attach the tabs with 1 hole, then the tabs with 2 holes, and so on).

f. Tape the edges of your shape to make sure the glue can dry properly (Figure B).

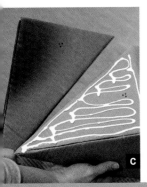

Fig. A: Cut cardboard pieces and leave the pattern until you've made the creases. Fig. B: Fold and glue each piece, taping in place until the glue dries.

Fig. C: Glue all the pieces together on matching surfaces. Fig. D: Tape the chair together while the glue dries. Fig. E: Gel medium and fabric make beautiful "upholstery."

4. Assemble your chair.

a. Once the glue has dried, carefully remove the tape from all your pieces.

b. Using the punched holes as your guide (the surfaces with matching holes will connect), glue the shapes together (Figure C).

You may find it easier to glue a few together and let them dry a bit before continuing. As you go, tape the edges together to hold the pieces in place (Figure D).

c. After the glue has dried, remove the tape and take a seat!

5. Decorate.

If you're into simplicity, Foldschool furniture looks super cool as-is. However, if you're like me, you won't be able to resist doing a bit of customization! Here are some fun ideas to get you started.

a. Decoupage your chairs using paper and gel medium (available from art supply stores). The great thing about gel medium is that it acts as both glue and varnish and will even give your chair some degree of waterproofing. It's water-based, nontoxic, and completely clear when dry.

b. Upholster your chairs with gel medium and fun fabrics (Figure E). Any fabric will work as long as it's not stretchy. I used some very thin, vintage kimono fabric, as well as a thicker, contemporary Japanese fabric, and both worked great.

You don't have to turn under the edges of your fabric since the gel will seal it and prevent fraying. Spread a thin layer of gel medium, place the fabric, and let it dry before spreading another layer over the top of the fabric.

c. Reduce the pattern by half and make doll-sized chairs. You don't need as much cardboard, and it'll give those plushy pals a place to sit at tea parties!

d. Give some markers and crayons to the kids, and just stand back and watch!

Anna Dilemna is a doll maker and freelance writer who has lived in New York City, Santiago, Chile, and Tokyo, Japan. Currently she lives in Switzerland and eats a lot of cheese. Her website is at annadilemna.typepad.com.

BUSINESS REPLY MAIL

FIRST-CLASS MAIL   PERMIT NO 865   NORTH HOLLYWOOD CA

POSTAGE WILL BE PAID BY ADDRESSEE

Craft:

PO BOX 17046
NORTH HOLLYWOOD CA 91615-9588

BUSINESS REPLY MAIL

FIRST-CLASS MAIL   PERMIT NO 865   NORTH HOLLYWOOD CA

POSTAGE WILL BE PAID BY ADDRESSEE

Craft:

PO BOX 17046
NORTH HOLLYWOOD CA 91615-9588

Sneaky Sleeve Pocket

Stick a secret compartment inside your jacket for hush items you want to stash. BY CY TYMONY

Sometimes your regular jacket pockets just won't do for some of your private, sneaky items you'd rather not have discovered. You can make a secret pocket easily enough for one of your spare jackets. Better yet, make a secret sleeve pocket that provides quick access and is custom made for your personal items, such as a pen, calculator, mini camera, voice recorder, flashlight, animal repellent, or personal alarm.

This project shows how to make a compact pocket for an iPod, from material that matches the jacket color. It's affixed with velcro stick-ons, allowing for easy removal prior to traveling and for cleaning purposes. Your secret pocket can be any size you desire. Just follow the basic design example given.

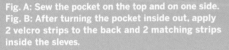
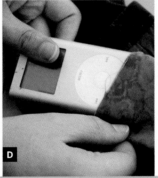

Fig. A: Sew the pocket on the top and on one side.
Fig. B: After turning the pocket inside out, apply
2 velcro strips to the back and 2 matching strips
inside the sleves.

Fig. C: Press the pocket in place. Fig. D: Slip the iPod
into the pocket and pinch the bottom corners together.
Fig. E: Press the pocket's small velcro strips together
to form a latch.

Materials

» **Jacket**
» **Cloth material** to match jacket
» **Stick-on velcro strips** 3 sets total
» **Needle and thread**
» **Scissors**

1. Snip and sew.

Cut a 6"×6" piece of cloth. Fold the cloth in half and
sew along the top and side border but leave the
bottom open (Figure A). Then turn the pocket inside
out. Ensure that the item fits properly inside the
pocket without being too snug; you want it to slide out
when it's mounted in the jacket sleeve upside down.

2. Stick.

Adhere two ½" velcro strips near the top and
bottom of the back of the pocket. Then adhere
2 matching velcro strips to the jacket's inside
lower sleeve area (Figure D). Next, apply 2 small ½"
velcro strips (1 soft strip and 1 hard velcro strip so

they latch together) to the bottom corners of the
open end of the pocket. Press the pocket in place
(Figure C).

3. Slide.

Slip the desired item (in this case an iPod) into
the pocket, which is mounted in the jacket sleeve
upside down (Figure D). Pinch the bottom corners
together; they'll act as a latch to hold the item in
the pocket (Figure E). Even when shaken, the item
shouldn't fall out.

4. Sneak.

With your arm by your side, you can use your little
finger to secretly pry open the pocket latch, and the
iPod will slide into the palm of your hand like magic.

Now you can have small, mostly flat items, like a
drive, mounted securely on the jacket and available
any time you need them.

Cy Tymony is a computer specialist and technical writer with
five books under his belt. sneakyuses.com

Duck Duck iPod

Make a fun yet durable iPod case with simple duck (or duct) tape. BY STEPHANIE MALLARD

Photography by Sam Murphy

Duck tape fascinates me. The sticky, tough, permanent tape is great, and crafting with it is even better. Before the "stuff that holds the world together" was invented, tape was not permanent. Tape was clear, breakable, and temporary. But in 1942, Johnson and Johnson invented a permanent tape that actually stuck! The world rejoiced. Since then, duck tape has been used on army Jeeps, guns, spacecraft, and the humble home air conditioning duct. Many have used it creatively as a material to make things like prom dresses, ties, wallets, and bracelets.

The idea of a duck tape iPod case started in the back seat of a long car ride to San Antonio. I had my iPod and a roll of gray duck tape (originally and often still referred to as "duck," not "duct"). So I put 2 and 2 together, and the duck tape iPod case was born.

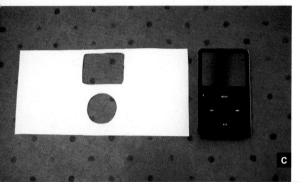
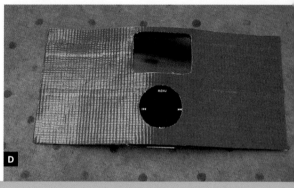

Fig. A: Make the duck tape sandwich.
Fig. B: Trim and transfer the pattern to the sandwich.

Fig. C: Cut the holes.
Fig. D: Compare the holes to the iPod.

Materials

» **Roll of duck tape** Many colors are available at duckproducts.com.
» **Sharp scissors**
» **Template** Print it out from craftzine.com/06/hide_duck.
» **X-Acto knife**
» **iPod**

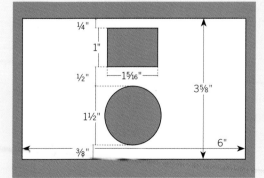

1. Make a duck tape sandwich.

Cut 2 pieces of duck tape, each a little more than double the width of your iPod. Join them into 1 by sticking the long edges together, then place on a flat surface, sticky side up. Repeat with 2 more pieces of duck tape, and stick these on top of the first 2, sticky side down. You've now got your sandwich, with non-sticky sides facing out and all the sticky stuff in the middle (Figure A).

2. Trim to fit.

Measure your duck sandwich's height by wrapping it around your iPod once and making sure it's tall enough. Once you've got the measurement, trim the top and bottom edges to fit.

3. Cut windows for the click wheel and screen.

Print the template, cut it out, and tape it onto your sandwich (Figure B).

NOTE: The template offered for this article at craftzine.com/06/hide_duck is for an iPod mini. For any other iPod, just measure the click wheel and screen and adjust accordingly.

E F

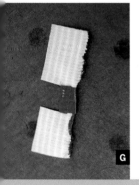

G H I

Fig. E: Wrap the sandwich around your iPod.
Fig. F: Slip the iPod into its cozy.
Fig. G: A completed tab.

Fig. H: Secure 2 tabs to the bottom of the iPod.
Fig. I: Secure 1 tab to the top of the iPod.

With an X-Acto knife, cut out the windows for the click wheel and screen (Figure C). Compare it against your iPod to make sure the windows match up (Figure D). Wrap it around your iPod to check the width, then tape the 2 loose edges of the duck tape together with a thin strip of duck tape, forming a sleeve (Figure E).

Slide the iPod inside the sleeve and make sure it's a tight fit, but loose enough that your iPod doesn't get stuck (Figure F)!

❋ TIP: To prevent the tape from sticking to the iPod, stick another piece of duck tape to the inside of the cozy, lengthwise to cover the seam.

4. Add securing straps.

Cut a small strip of duck tape and make 2 slits of the same length in the same side (Figure G). Fold and stick the middle piece down, and trim. You now have a strap! Make 3 of these and stick 2 of them onto the bottom of the case, to hold the iPod in (Figure H). Stick the remaining tab onto the top of the case. This tab can be opened or shut (Figure I).

Voilà! You now have your duck tape cozy creation.

Sometimes your creativity may feel a little limited by the duck tape color options. You can personalize your iPod cover by adhering paper to the outside of the duck tape. I also make iPod cases with paper and packing tape (notice the cover of *CRAFT, Volume 01* in the example on the left). To see how to make these, go to craftzine.com/06/hide_duck.

Stephanie Mallard, 13, is a beginning engineering artist who makes creative things with convenient materials. She has earned a reputation at her middle school as the "Duck Tape Kid" for duck-taping her binder, folders, and agenda to improve the designs. She lives in Texas with her mom, dad, cat, and dog.

Photography (inset) by Stephanie Mallard

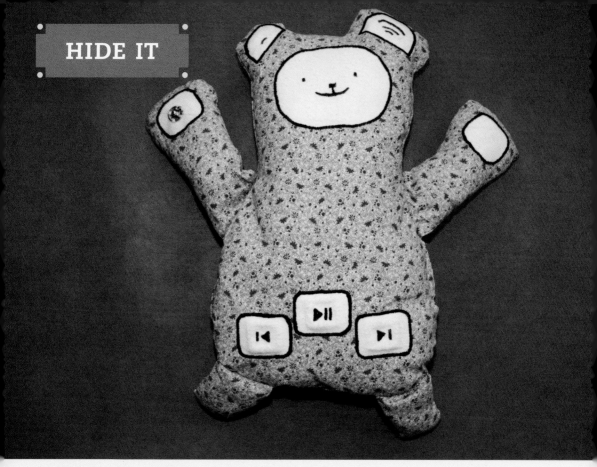

Teddy Bear Remote Control

*You'll always fight over the remote
when it's this cuddly.* BY LEAH CULVER

S oft electronics? The phrase seems quite contradictory. Electronics are a combination of hard plastic and metal, anything but soft and cuddly. However, after stumbling across some conductive thread on the internet, I was inspired to attempt my own soft electronics. Apparently conductive thread is used to repair electric lamés worn by fencers, but it can also be used for some creative circuitry.

The teddy bear remote was the first project I made with my coveted spool of conductive thread, and it's an adorable way to control an iPod or computer. The bear is a modification to a standard radio frequency (RF) remote control and is surprisingly soft. If you're daring enough to sew and solder, the teddy bear remote is functional, cuddly, and fun to make.

Photograph by Sam Murphy

Materials

- » **Conductive thread**
- » **Griffin RF (radio frequency) remote control** Any model will do.
- » **Soldering iron and solder**
- » **Sewing machine, thread, pins, and needles**
- » **Fabric (3 varieties)** floral print, plain colored, and white muslin
- » **Hook and eye fasteners, size 0**
- » **Snap fastener**
- » **Velcro**
- » **Sticky-back fusible web**
- » **Cotton or polyester stuffing**
- » **Conductive metal tape** found at hardware stores in the plumbing section
- » **¼"-thick foam tape** found at hardware stores
- » **Permanent or fabric marker**

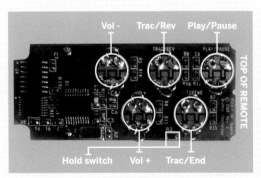

Vol -   Trac/Rev   Play/Pause

TOP OF REMOTE

Hold switch   Vol +   Trac/End

1. Solder fasteners to the remote.

Carefully disassemble the remote control (Figure A, on next page). The circuit board is nicely labeled and has 5 buttons and a hold switch (see the shiny circles above). You'll need to solder the eye fasteners onto the circuit board as shown in the image above, so the thread can be tied to something. The right half of each button dot provides its power and the left half connects to its specific function, so any right half can be connected to the left half to activate that function.

The on/hold switch is a bit trickier. When the arms of the bear are snapped together, the remote will be switched on. The switch has 3 contacts: 1 for "on," 1 for "hold," and 1 shared contact that connects to either "on" or "hold" via the switch. Push the switch into the "hold" position (toward the top of the remote control) and solder 1 eye to the "on" contact and 1 to the shared contact. (We won't connect to the "hold" contact since the bear doesn't use this functionality.) It's important to arrange the eye fasteners so that the conductive threads won't cross.

2. Sew a circuit.

Draw a pattern on a piece of paper for a bear body, arms, and legs, about ¾" larger than you want the finished bear. Cut out your fabric pieces using your patterns, and cut out the muslin fabric in the same shape as the body. Design a face and use the fusible web to attach it to the front of the bear.

Place your remote control circuit board on top of the piece of muslin in a strategic position such as the bear's armpit, for access to the battery. On the muslin, mark where the buttons will go. Tie a piece of conductive thread to an eye fastener on the circuit board and then sew it across the muslin to the button location. Doubling the thread ensures that if one breaks, the other will still make the button function. Repeat for each side of each button and the on/hold switch. Leave plenty of extra thread for the switch since it will go to the bear's arms.

Using the fusible web, attach the muslin to the back of the front piece of the bear (Figure B). The fusible web makes the fabric stiffer, so attach only a few points on the muslin to the front piece to hold them together, and keep the threads from crossing.

After the muslin circuit has been attached, mark on the front where the buttons should be placed. At each button location, place 2 rectangles of conductive tape, 1 for each connecting side of the circuit, about ¹⁄₁₆" apart (Figure C). Then stitch each conductive thread over its piece of tape so that the thread touches the conductive part of the tape. The threads for the on/hold switch don't need to be attached to anything for now, but be careful not to cross them as this will drain the battery.

3. Make buttons.

To make the sewn button icons, draw the designs on paper with pencil, rub them onto the fabric, then darken them with a marking pen. Sew the outlines, then fill in by hand-sewing and using a permanent marker to fix mistakes (Figure E).

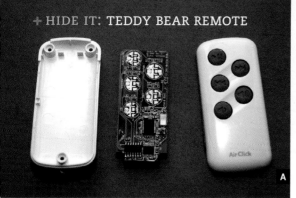
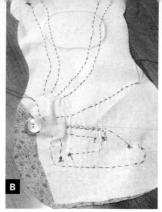
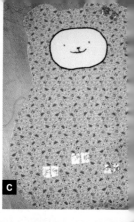

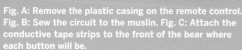

Fig. A: Remove the plastic casing on the remote control. Fig. B: Sew the circuit to the muslin. Fig. C: Attach the conductive tape strips to the front of the bear where each button will be.

Fig. D: Create buttons using conductive tape and foam, and then test them by placing each one on its correct spot. Fig. E: Finish the buttons by sewing a border around each one.

If the custom buttons seem a bit difficult, you could use printed icons on iron-on inkjet T-shirt transfer paper, or draw the icons onto the buttons with a permanent marker or fabric marker.

Next, cut out the buttons with an icon in the center of each. Attach a square of conductive tape to the back of each button, and cut out a fat border of adhesive foam to fit around each conductive tape square. Test each button by placing it in the correct spot on the front of the bear (Figure D).

Place fusible web on the back of each button, around the outer edge only, and press onto the correct place on the front of the bear. Finish by sewing a border around each button.

4. Create bear arms.

Next make the bear's arms, which also function as the on switch. Cut out the arms and attach the inner paw decoration, as you did with the face. Sew one part of a metal snap fastener to the inside of one paw and the other to the outside of the other paw.

Sew the 2 sides of each arm together, reverse, and stuff each with cotton or polyester stuffing. Before stuffing, run the conductive threads corresponding to each arm through the arm and tie securely around

the snap part. Both snap parts should now connect to the sewn circuit by the conductive thread, with the arms hanging loosely from the bear body.

5. Assemble the bear body.

Cut out the bear legs, sew together, reverse, and stuff. Pin the arms and legs onto the front of the bear, pointing inward, and place the back of the bear on top, with the right sides of the fabric facing each other. Pin in place and sew completely around the bear, leaving only a 2" gap near the circuit board.

Turn right side out, remove the pins, and stuff. Add extra stuffing between the circuit board and the front of the bear. Finally, sew velcro on the inside of the gap for changing the battery.

Leah Culver is a software developer living in San Francisco. She enjoys sewing, solving crossword puzzles, and working on her website, pownce.com.

Photography by Sam Murphy and Leah Culver (Figures B and C)

Pantyhose Petals

Create delicate nylon flowers to dress up a wedding gown, veil, or centerpiece. BY MARY BETH KLATT

In the 1950s, women had to wear hosiery to the office or risk being fired. Naturally, these ladies ended up with a lot of ripped and snagged pantyhose. Although some tossed these ruined pairs, the crafty ones cooked up beautiful ways to reuse them. Many women ended up dyeing and cutting them up to create flowers for wedding veils, corsages, and hats.

Now those same flowers will set you back a small fortune on eBay, but you can re-create them for a fraction of the price, and get a vintage look that would be appropriate on Elizabeth Taylor in *Father of the Bride*.

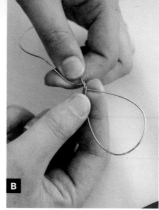

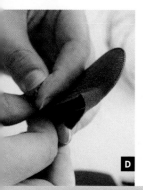

Fig. A: Make a loop of wire for the petal's frame. Fig. B: Twist the wire together at the base to form the stem. Fig. C: Cut out petals from the nylon pantyhose. Fig. D: Cover the petal with hose material.

Fig. E: Tape the base with green floral tape. Fig. F: Voilà! One petal complete. Now make a couple more.

Materials

- » **Pair of pantyhose or sheer tights** Any color will work. My favorites are pink, light blue, gold, pale yellow, and fuchsia.
- » **Floral tape**
- » **Jewelry wire** I like a crimped silver wire for an authentic look, but here I used plain copper.
- » **Wire cutters**
- » **Stamens** You can find these in the wedding aisle at your local craft supply store. I bought white ones and dabbed them with nail polish to antique them.
- » **Faux leaves** Also in the wedding aisle.

1. Cut and crimp.

Cut approximately 9" of wire — you can always shorten it later. You can also crimp the wire with your fingers for visual interest. To do this, hold the wire in both hands and use your thumbnails to indent the wire. Alternate sides, indenting just where the petal will be, which is the middle portion of the wire. You don't need to do this for the stem.

2. Frame your petal with wire.

Bend the middle of the wire into a petal shape (Figure A). We are making 1 petal now, which we'll repeat several times to create a flower in the end. A 2"-wide petal is a good place to start, although I've made smaller. When you get a loop size you like, twist the wire together at the base, forming the stem (Figure B).

3. Cut the pantyhose.

Discard the girdle and feet, but save the legs. Snip the legs into 4"×4" squares (Figure C). You can also make larger squares for larger petals.

4. Add nylon to your petal frame.

While holding the petal and nylon in your hand, gently tug the hose over the wire petal, joining the corners together and bunching all the raw edges at the base (Figure D). Gently bend the loop to shape your petal. The idea is to make the fabric as taut as

G H

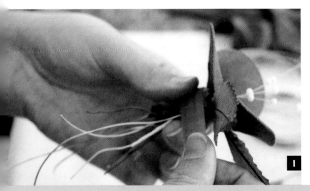

I J

Fig. G: Insert the stamens into the middle of the petal trio. Fig. H: Tighten the stem, taking care to cover any exposed wire and raw edges.

Fig. I. Attach the leaves and bind the entire stem with floral tape. Fig. J: Something blue, ready for a wedding or two.

possible at the petal's outer edge, and fuller toward the center.

5. Secure your petal.

When you're happy with the way your petal looks, secure the base with 2"–3" of wire. To do this, position the middle of the wire strip at the petal base and wrap it around a few times. Line up the 2 wire ends that will make your stem (see Figure F for finished wire detail). Carefully trim the excess hose, making sure not to cut it too close to the wire. Now wrap the base a few times with floral tape to make sure the nylon is secure.

6. Create a trio of petals.

Using the previous instructions, make 2 more petals (you can make more petals if you desire a more intricate blossom, but too many can be difficult to manage).

7. Let your petals bloom.

Take several stamens (I used 3) and insert them into the middle of your petal trio (Figure G). Use the tape to secure the group, taking care again to cover any exposed wire or raw edges (Figure H). Add some

faux leaves and fasten with tape (Figures I and J). Try different colors!

8. Wrap your stem.

Beginning at the base, wrap your stem with floral tape, being sure to cover any raw edges or wire (Figure E). Continue all the way down the stem, molding the tape to the wire.

Mary Beth Klatt is a Chicago writer who frequently writes about fashion and design. In her spare time, she loves to sew, knit, and crochet (not all at the same time).

T-Shirt Wedding Dress

Have a dazzlingly white wedding day.

BY DONNA KROIZ AND LAUREN KROIZ

Until the late 19th century, brides generally bought the fanciest dress they could afford and then wore it throughout their marriage as an evening gown. With the rise of mass-produced clothing, white became the popular color — maximally impractical, it signified the owner would wear the dress only once. Efficient women often married in white and then dyed their dresses to wear again.

In the 21st century, there's no need to choose between anti-consumerist values and looking cute in white on your wedding day. Learn how to make an adorable, versatile dress using white cotton T-shirts — comfortable, repurposed, and perfect for years of reuse.

Photography by Lauren Kroiz

Materials

- » **White T-shirts** several, depending on pattern and size
- » **Thread**
- » **Sewing machine**
- » **Fabric scissors**
- » **Pins** straight and/or safety
- » **Dress pattern** (choose any you like)
- » **Notions, zipper, buttons, etc.** as called for by your pattern
- » **Sewing machine knit needle (optional)**

1. Create or select a pattern for your dress.

If using a commercial pattern, pick one appropriate for jersey fabric. If creating your own pattern, remember T-shirt fabric is soft and has some stretch, so it will look best draped and loosely fitted.

❋ TIP: **Showing this pattern to people will help you collect T-shirts from those fearful of seeing you married in a pile of rags.**

2. Collect white T-shirts.

The number of T-shirts you'll need depends on many factors, including how damaged the shirts are, the size of the person who gave them to you, what pattern you select, and how big you are! Having extra shirts is a great idea and will make the project easier to complete. Our experience indicates you should allow at least 6 men's medium-sized shirts for each yard of fabric required by your pattern.

Wash the shirts in hot water and tumble dry to preshrink the fabric. Use bleach or another type of fabric whitener to help ensure that each shirt is the same shade of white. This is especially important if you've collected the shirts from a variety of people. Iron each shirt so that you can easily distinguish stains and holes from wrinkles.

3. Check for stains and holes.

Lay out your shirts in a clean and very, very well-lit space. A table set up outside or under natural light is vital, especially if you'll have an outdoor ceremony. Be sure to check that each shirt is approximately the same shade of white to ensure your finished dress won't look patchy or yellowed.

Mark each stain and hole you find with straight or safety pins (Figure A). Turn each shirt over and examine the back. Mark these holes and stains separately. (Be sure that your pins go through only 1 layer of the shirt.) This is a good time to find a fastidious friend for a second set of eyes.

4. Deconstruct the shirts.

Remove the sleeves and the collar of each shirt. Cut around the stains and holes you marked, salvaging the biggest pieces you can from each shirt (Figure B). Save the scraps to use as rags. Identify symmetrical pieces (Figure C); our dress improved when we created a V pattern in the skirt by lining up symmetrical sections of shirt. Begin cutting T-shirt sections to fit pattern pieces.

Be careful to keep the sections oriented so that the grain line of the fabric runs vertically from the collar to the bottom hem of the shirt. You may arrange the pieces with the grain on the horizontal or vertical axis. Don't place the sections so that the grain falls on a diagonal (this will make your dress hang differently), and avoid mixing sections with vertical and horizontal grain, which may create uneven stretching and bagging.

5. Examine the pattern.

Depending on your modesty, you may want to use 2 layers of T-shirt. We used 2 in the bodice of the dress, and used a slip for the skirt. Identify the pattern pieces for which you'll need multiple layers, and duplicate them in paper. If dress pattern pieces are small enough, you may want to use 1 big T-shirt section. Not only does this reduce the sewing for you, but it's ideal in sections such as the bodice of your dress, where you want construction details, such as gathering, to be the focus.

❋ TIP: **Consider patchwork as a kind of decoration that adds visual volume to your dress body. You can use it strategically when designing your own dress.**

Fit the remaining T-shirt sections to the remaining larger pattern pieces. To save time, arrange your pieces so that the bottom hem of the dress is constructed from the bottom hems of the shirts (Figure E). Though it may be a bit tricky, it creates

A B

C D E

Fig. A: In strong light, identify stains and mark them with pins. Fig. B: Dismantle the shirts, cutting around seams and stains. Fig. C: Lay out symmetrical pattern pieces and sections of clean fabric. Fig. D: Using a zigzag stitch, piece together fabric to fill each pattern piece. (This example uses black thread for visibility. Use white or a pastel shade for a less "punk rock" look.) Fig. E: Align bottoms of the tees to create the bottom hem of the dress.

a polished look that can be otherwise difficult to achieve without a serger. If you can't arrange your sections to utilize the existing hems, try using a fusible interfacing to stabilize the fabric, and practice several times before attempting to finish the hem of your dress. You may reconsider!

6. Sew the dress.

Pin the sections to the pattern. Be sure to allow for at least ½" overlap if you're piecing the sections together. Move to the sewing machine. When sewing the T-shirt sections together, both piecing and seaming, it's important to avoid stretching the material or you'll end up with uneven puckering. If you get skipped stitches or see holes in your fabric, try a new needle or a stretch needle.

Stitch together the sections that make up each pattern piece using white thread. Slightly overlap the sections about ¼" and use a small zigzag stitch along the edge of that overlap (Figure D). This will both attach the section and finish the edge, because the T-shirt fabric, unlike a woven fabric, is not likely to unravel.

Practice seaming with scrap T-shirt fabric. Knits are often easily torn apart at the seam, so it's

important to choose an appropriate stitch. We used 2 parallel straight seams to prevent the 2 pieces from tearing apart. You can also use a zigzag stitch, but be careful to reduce its length so it doesn't sew through when the seam is stretched.

Your machine may also have a setting for a stretch stitch, used specifically for sewing knits, but be aware this seam will be very difficult to remove so you should baste-stitch the seam first.

Sew the sections together following the pattern instructions. Be sure to check the fit several times throughout construction as the T-shirt sections may have more or less stretch than you imagine!

7. Have a beautiful wedding.

Afterward, store the dress to show your children, or follow women of a previous era and color your dress with any cotton dye to wear again and again.

Donna Kroiz is a Virginia-based seamstress. She eloped in jeans and a polyester shirt. It was the 70s. Her daughter Lauren Kroiz is a Los Angeles-based crafter raised to believe that everyone has the right to enter into whatever union they want wearing whatever they like. ticklishtortoise.com

Fig Wine

Skip the vineyards and make a rich, tasty wine you can't buy at the store. BY ALASTAIR BLAND

Photography by Sam Murphy

G rape wine is fine and good, but for something you'll never find at the grocery store, sip this: fig wine. The thing is, you've got to make it yourself.

I've made wine from several varieties of figs, fresh and dried, but I've made it best from dried organic Calimyrna figs, tawny brown fruits that come crusted in a thick layer of natural sugar. (Turkish Smyrna figs are a fine, if not local, stand-in.) The wine these figs produce — of rich amber shades and whiskey, caramel, and tobacco flavors — can be drunk in just 2 or 3 months, and the word on the web says that fig wine has the potential to improve in the bottle for years.

Materials

» **1lb dried figs**
» **2lbs white sugar**
» **1gal water**
» **1 packet Windsor Ale yeast
   or Champagne yeast**
» **¼tsp powdered grape tannin**
» **3tsp granulated ascorbic acid**
» **1tsp yeast nutrient**
» **Large stainless steel cook pots (2)**
   2- or 3-gallon
» **Nylon fine-mesh sack**
» **Glass carboys (2)** 1-, 3-, or 5-gallon
» **Rubber stopper and airlock**
» **5' rubber hose**
» **Bottling stick and siphon pump**
   from the homebrew shop
» **Used beer bottles** Get standard
   pry-off bottles; twist-off bottles
   will not work.
» **Caps**
» **Bottle capper**
» **Iodine equipment sanitizer**

✳ TIPS

» Starting a batch of fig wine takes just an hour or less, but considering the months you'll spend waiting while it ages, it will be worth your while to make 3 or 5 gallons. Simple math can adjust this 1 gallon recipe for larger quantities.

» Cleanliness is of key importance in making good wine, but keep dish soap away. You'll need 2 cooking pots for this recipe. Boil and dump ½gal of water to cleanse them of soapsuds. One of these pots will serve as your fermentation vessel.

» Figs cannot be juiced, so tap water must be added, along with sugar, the amount of which will directly determine the final alcohol content. Using 2¼lbs of sugar per gallon of water will produce a wine in the 12% alcohol range. This fig wine recipe calls for a lot of figs, and so I've reduced the sugar addition to 2lbs.

» A trip to the local homebrew and winemaking shop will supply you with the specialized equipment and ingredients you need, like powdered grape tannin, granulated ascorbic acid, yeast nutrient, and yeast. It shouldn't run you more than 50 bucks or so, and the products will serve you through many batches of wine. If you don't live near a beer/winemaking shop, try midwestsupplies.com.

1. Fill your 2 pots partway with water, cover each with a lid, and heat them to a boil. After 20 minutes, dump the water. They should now be clean. If not, repeat the process.

2. Set one pot aside for the moment, while you use the other to heat ½gal of water to about 200°F.

3. Finely dice the dried figs and toss them into the not-quite-boiling water. Using a clean fork or potato masher, stir and smash the figs. Pulp them beyond recognition, working them until the water is a dark, deep brown, and all the figs are completely annihilated.

4. Now, ask for assistance from a friend and pour the water slowly through the nylon sack and into the other pot. Add another ¼gal of cold tap water to the heap of cooked figs, stir again, and again strain the juice through the sack. Repeat once more with the last ¼gal of water. This time dump all the figs into the sack, tie it off securely, and drop it into the pot.

5. Add the grape tannin, granulated ascorbic acid, and yeast nutrient.

6. Cover the pot with a towel, and when it has cooled to approximately 90°F, add 1tsp of yeast. Cover the pot again.

7. At room temperature, the stew will come roiling to life within a day or so — the fragrant miracle of fermentation. Slosh the pot on occasion to keep it well aerated. Otherwise, keep it covered with a towel.

8. After 7 to 10 days, fermentation will subside. The wine will grow still and calm as the sediment and expired yeast settle to the bottom.

Sanitize your glass carboy and rubber hose using water treated with iodine. Then fill the hose with tap water (to start the siphon action), dip one end gently into the wine, just under the surface, and slip the other end all the way to the bottom of the clean glass jug. Abruptly place the jug on the floor, and the elevation change will start the wine moving from

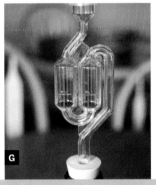

Fig. A: After dicing, dump the figs into the pot of hot water. Fig. B: Mash thoroughly. Fig. C: Pour the dark "fig juice" through a nylon mesh bag into your second pot. Fig. D: Fill the bag with the fig pieces, tie off, and add to the pot of fig juice. Fig. E: Keep covered until fermentation has subsided — about a week. Fig. F: Siphon the wine into a clean gallon jug. Fig. G: Remove the stopper only during racking. Fig. H: At last! The bottles are capped!

cook pot, or *primary fermenter*, through the tube and into the glass jug, or *secondary fermenter*.

9. Siphon off all the wine you can without drawing up any of the waste matter, then plug the filled carboy with a rubber stopper and airlock, both sanitized by boiling, and leave the wine in a cool, dark place.

Sediment will drop to the bottom as the wine clears. After 1 month, siphon the wine (not the sediment) into your other clean glass jug. This is called *racking* your wine. Allow 1 more month. Rack again into the first jug.

10. After 1 more month, bottle it. Sanitize your bottles either by treating with iodine or by rinsing them with water and then baking them in the oven at 200°F for 1 hour. Allow them to cool on the floor, 3' below the wine.

Meanwhile, rinse out your siphon pump and bottling stick with hot water and iodine sanitizer before rigging up to your hose. Always being careful not to stir up the sediment, dip the pump into the wine and the stick into the first bottle, and start filling.

(The bottling stick is a clever little contraption — you'll see how to use it. And the siphon pump is not entirely necessary — it just makes life a little easier.) Boil the caps for 90 seconds before capping the bottles securely one by one.

11. Mark the date on the bottles with a permanent marker and stash them in a cool, dark place, like a basement closet. Sample a bottle after 6 months, then stash again. Continue to make more fig wine, stockpiling great quantities for long-term aging and occasional tasting at dinner parties.

You can count on it: The vineyards of the Earth will never disappear, and your guests will always show up at your door with old-fashioned grape wine, but the fig wine is up to you.

Alastair Bland is a journalist in San Francisco. He can be reached through his blog at alastairbland.blogspot.com.

Beautiful Beans

Natto could deter heart disease and revolutionize your breakfast. BY ERIC SMILLIE

Stinky and sticky, natto would be disgusting if it weren't so delicious — or so good for you. Though still hard to find in the United States, this fermented soybean recently hit food fad status in Japan, where it has been made for centuries.

Research suggests that eating natto and *Bacillus subtilis*, the bacteria that creates it, breaks down blood clots to encourage circulation, boosts the immune system, helps prevent osteoporosis, and encourages healthy digestion. Thanks to the magic of fermentation, the bacteria produces fungicidal antibiotics that defend the precious, slimy jewels from spoilage, while it breaks down proteins and soluble sugars into easily digestible forms that cancel out unwanted performances by the musical fruit.

Photography by Eric Smillie

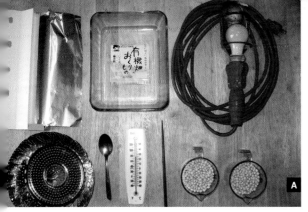

Fig. A: Your materials (minus the pot). Fig. B: Wash the beans and soak fully submerged in water for up to 24 hours. Fig. C: Steam until the beans are soft. Some recipes demand that the beans be inoculated immediately while still hot, but I know one fanatic fermenter who finds this unnecessary. Fig. D: Mix the commercial natto with your beans and spread in a glass dish. Mail-order spores will have their own instructions.

Materials

- » **2 cups dried soybeans**
- » **1 package commercial natto or appropriate dose of spores** Japan's organic produce seal bears the green letters "JAS" and a leaf in a triple circle.
- » **Water**
- » **Large pot with lid**
- » **Metal steamer basket**
- » **Glass baking dish**
- » **Aluminum foil**
- » **Spoon**
- » **Chopstick**
- » **Oven**
- » **Incandescent work light**
- » **Thermometer**

Fresh natto is hard to come by in the U.S. "I'm the only kid on the block," explains Charles Kendall of the Kendall Food Company in Worthington, Mass., which is likely the country's only commercial producer. If you don't live in the Northeast and don't plan on visiting Japan, you'll just have to pick up a frozen package at a specialty grocery store or order the bacteria from GEM Cultures (gemcultures.com) and grow your own.

1. Soak.
Wash dust and dirt from the beans and remove any that are discolored. Soak fully submerged in water for 12 to 24 hours until they're swollen (Figure B).

2. Steam.
Drain the beans and give them another rinse for good measure. Fill the pot with water to just below the steamer bed. Put in the beans, cover, and steam until they are soft enough to crush easily but are not yet bursting on their own (Figure C). In a regular pot, this can take 5 or 6 hours. Replenish with ½ cup boiling water every hour. A pressure cooker shortens this time to 45 minutes.

3. Sterilize.
When the beans are ready, sterilize the baking dish and the spoon with boiling water, vodka, or another strong alcohol.

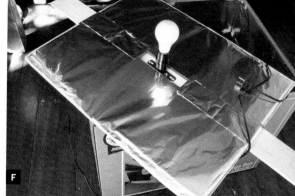

Fig. E: You can home-ferment in an oven with a worklight for heat. Fig. F: If your oven is too warm, you can make a fermenter from a cardboard box lined in foil; a lightbulb is suspended from the lid.

Fig. G: Every 6 hours, remove the foil and inspect your beans. Finished beans will look dried and wrinkled. Fig. H: You should see telltale white, sticky strings when you lift a spoonful up from the mixture.

4. Inoculate.

Pour the beans into the baking dish. Mix in 2–3 Tbsp of commercial natto, and spread the beans evenly across the dish (Figure D). Carefully cover with a sheet of foil, and punch air holes in the surface. Some recipes suggest adding sugar or salt, or a bit of the bean water if the mixture seems dry. Mine turned out fine without any of these additions.

5. Ferment.

The natto bacteria must now grow at about 104°F. If you have a modern oven, place the baking dish on its top shelf, next to your thermometer. Put the work light on the oven floor, turn it on, and close the door (Figure E). Every hour, check the temperature. You may have to change the wattage of your bulb or prop the door open to get it right. Don't worry if the temperature fluctuates; I've hit as high as 122° and as low as 95° before leveling out at 104°.

If, like me, your oven runs too hot or you can't trust your roommates to leave it alone, use a cardboard box or a cooler instead (Figure F). Or adopt the style of Yoko Kondo, who ferments and pickles food for Minako Organic, her Japanese restaurant in San Francisco. Ever since she was a student in

Japan, Kondo has wrapped her foil-covered baking dish in 3 bath towels and left it out to ferment for a full day in direct sunlight. In the winter, she puts the package in her bed under the covers.

6. Test.

Every 6 hours, remove the foil and inspect your beans (Figure G). Finished beans will have dried, darkened, and wrinkled on the surface, and should give off a light aroma of ammonia. Pull up a spoonful with a sterilized spoon, and you should see the telltale white, sticky strings (Figure H). If you haven't achieved these results after about 24 hours, something likely went wrong. Cover and store successful natto in the refrigerator for 1–2 days to let its flavor develop. It will last for 2 weeks in the fridge, and the bacteria can survive frozen for 2 months.

7. Eat.

Natto is traditionally served at breakfast, mixed with rice, spicy mustard, soy sauce, and chopped green onions.

When he isn't playing with rotting food, Eric Smillie writes for magazines.

Photograph by Jen Siska

Super Simple Circle Skirt

Avoid the hassle of hems by using a vintage tablecloth to make a perfect skirt. BY ERIN MCKEAN

There are lots of things to love about sewing: the pleasure of choosing just the right fabric for just the right pattern, the feel of sharp scissors carving out the pattern pieces, the hiss of the hot iron pressing a perfect seam ... but there are not-so-lovable parts, too. One of my least favorite parts of sewing is hemming, and I'm always looking for ways to make it easier or faster, or, if I'm lucky, to escape it entirely. One sure way to avoid hemming is to work with fabric that has been helpfully pre-hemmed by someone else — like a tablecloth.

Materials

- » **Tablecloth** I suggest buying a few cheap ones from yard sales as prototypes before cutting into Grandma's heirloom.
- » **Measuring tape**
- » **Fabric marking pencil** or chalk
- » **Pins**
- » **Sewing machine (optional)**
- » **Zipper, 8" or 10"**
- » **Single-fold bias tape** length = your waist measurement + 6"
- » **Scissors**
- » **Iron**
- » **Hook and eyes, button, or ribbon (optional)**
- » **Blue painter's tape (optional)**

It's easy, fun, and quick to make a circle skirt from a round tablecloth. Tablecloths come in great colors and prints. You can buy them cheap at yard sales, online, and at discount stores, and they're often 100% cotton. I prefer to work with tablecloths at least 60" in diameter, but you can find one that will work at every length from "tutu" to "majestic floor-sweeper." And best of all, you'll avoid the most difficult part of making a circle skirt: hemming it.

1. Wash, dry, and iron tablecloth.

Wash and dry at the hottest settings, then iron with plenty of steam. You don't want to be surprised by any shrinkage later! For vintage tablecloths, wash, dry, and press as you would a finished skirt, then check carefully for any minor stains or holes, and decide where on the skirt you would want them to fall — the sides are usually the best place for a stain or small hole to be least noticeable. Mark them with blue painter's tape in a big X, so that you can't miss them when you start cutting. Also, cut off any labels!

2. Take one measurement.

To make a circle skirt from a tablecloth, you only need 1 measurement: your waist. To measure your waist for this project, pull the tape snugly around you, where you want the waist of your skirt to fall. You may want to measure a couple of times to make sure you have this number right.

3. One seam, or two?

Once you have your waist measurement, decide whether you'd like to have 1 side seam or 2. I prefer 2, so that I can put a pocket on the side opposite the zipper. These instructions are for a skirt with 2 seams; alter accordingly if you want just 1 seam. For each seam, leave 1" for the seam allowance.

Then comes the math: 30" waist, plus 2" (2 side seams), minus 1" (because the waist circle cut on the bias *will* stretch) = 31". And, if you remember your high school geometry, the formula for finding the radius of a circle when you know the circumference is to divide the circumference by 2π.

$31 / (2 * 3.142) = 4.93$

Round that to $4\frac{7}{8}$", and then subtract $\frac{1}{4}$" for the waistline seam to get a radius of $4\frac{5}{8}$". Find that on your measuring tape (Figure A).

4. Make a skirt doughnut.

Fold your tablecloth in half, and then in half again. Arrange the tablecloth carefully, making the hems even and smoothing out any wrinkles. Pin the zero mark of your measuring tape firmly at the pointy end of your tablecloth-pie (Figure B).

I like to cut a hole in my measuring tape at the right point and stick a pencil through it (Figure C) — that way I can mark the cutting line in one clean sweep.

Once your waistline is marked (Figure D), cut it out carefully (Figure E), and you'll have a big skirt

Photography by Erin McKean and Jen Siska (Figures I and J)

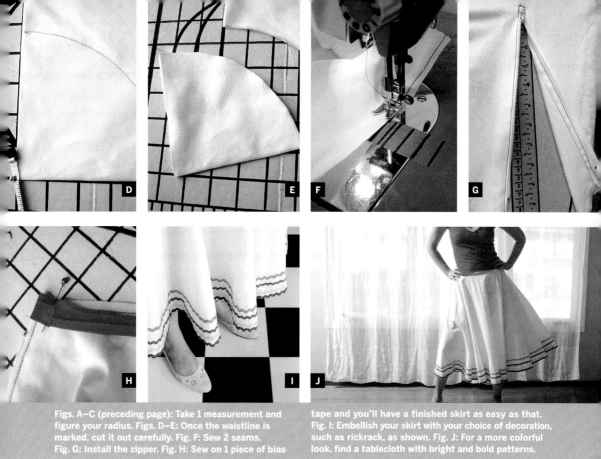

Figs. A–C (preceding page): Take 1 measurement and figure your radius. Figs. D–E: Once the waistline is marked, cut it out carefully. Fig. F: Sew 2 seams. Fig. G: Install the zipper. Fig. H: Sew on 1 piece of bias tape and you'll have a finished skirt as easy as that. Fig. I: Embellish your skirt with your choice of decoration, such as rickrack, as shown. Fig. J: For a more colorful look, find a tablecloth with bright and bold patterns.

doughnut. Then cut along the side folds to make 2 pieces. Note which piece you wanted for the front and which for the back, and mark the back with a pin or tape, or by writing in the seam allowance.

Now that you have 2 pieces, stitch along the waist about ¼" in (Figure F). This will help keep the waist from stretching while you work.

5. Sew the side seams and install the zipper.

Put your 2 skirt pieces right-side together, and sew the right-hand seam from the hem to the top. Align your zipper against the other side seam (zippers usually go on the left) and mark the bottom stopper. Then sew from the hem to that mark.

At this point *try on* your skirt! If it's too big, take in the side seams a bit, and if it's too small, let them out. Then press the seam open and install your zipper (Figure G) using your favorite method — there's a great lapped zipper tutorial from Fashion Incubator at craftzine.com/go/lapped and several tutorials from *Threads* magazine at taunton.com/threads.

6. Finish the waistband.

Open up one side of your single-fold bias tape and

sew it, right side to right side, along the waist edge of your skirt (Figure H). You should be sewing right on top of your staystitching line, about ¼" from the edge. Fold the bias tape to the inside, and then stitch again on the bias tape along the fold. Press to the inside of the skirt, and sew along the free edge of the bias tape with your machine (or finish by hand).

To finish the top of the waistband, you have several options. If your zipper is sturdy, just leave it as is! You can also fasten the top edge with a hook and eye, or use a decorative button and thread loop. Another cute waistline finish is to sew a piece of ribbon along the outside of the waistband, leaving 6"–8" extra at each end to tie in a bow.

Press your skirt one final time and you're done!

➕ For pockets, embellishments, and fit adjustments, see craftzine.com/06/stitch_circleskirt.

Erin McKean was editor of the *New Oxford American Dictionary*, 2nd Edition. She writes about dresses at her blog, A Dress A Day (dressaday.com).

Says James to Red Molly, my hat's off to you - it's a Vincent Black Lightning, 1952

And I've seen you at the corners and cafes, it seems

Red hair and black leather, my favourite colour scheme

And he pulled her on behind and down to Box Hill they did ride

Knitting Lyrical

Stitch a favorite song into your next sweater.

BY THEO WRIGHT

I have been designing and hand-knitting song lyrics for the last 20 years. I started knitting traditional Fair Isle patterns, and then discovered that the same technique is great for knitting words as well. So I started designing and making sweaters with song lyrics. I've made lots of mistakes, I've gradually improved my technique, and I've learned a lot on the way. This article is based on two recent examples: one sweater designed around Richard Thompson's "1952 Vincent Black Lightning" (a story of love, death, and most importantly, a motorbike), and the other around Tom Waits' "Dirt in the Ground" (a story of death, darkness, and despair). The same design and construction principles can be applied to any lyrics, poetry, or other words you might want to use.

Photography by Theo Wright

> » **4-ply wool** Colors and quantity will vary depending on your design.
> » **Spreadsheet software** or graph paper and pencil
> » **Tape measure**
> » **Scissors**
> » **Darning needle**
>
> **Knitting needles:**
> » **Pair 3.25mm (US size 3)** for the body
> » **Pair 2.75mm (US size 2)** for the rib

1. Choose a typeface.

You need a typeface that's suitable for knitting, and it's a lot quicker to use an existing one than to design your own. I use one already laid out on a grid from Sheila McGregor's *The Complete Book of Traditional Fair Isle Knitting*. Designing with text is essentially typesetting. There are probably whizzy bits of software designed specifically to help with this, but a spreadsheet works just fine.

If using software, format the cells so they are square, and then use the Shading ⇒ Color function to fill them. Keep in mind that each square cell represents 1 stitch. Blocking out each letter is a bit time-consuming, but you only need to do it once. Set up a page with your alphabet and maybe some words that you'll use a lot (Figure B), and just copy and paste them into a new worksheet to create new words and sentences for each new project. If you're seriously technophobic, just use graph paper instead.

2. Choose a song.

You're going to be wearing this sweater (or someone is), so the song had best be something you or they like. The quantity of lyrics can be a barrier. Don't attempt "Stuck Inside of Mobile with the Memphis Blues Again" unless you're knitting for someone who's XXXXL, and you've got a lot of time. It's better to choose 1 or 2 verses and display them really well than to try to fit everything in.

It's helpful to use words that make sense when someone tries to read them. Repetition and non-sense words sound great in songs but don't work particularly well in print or when knitted. Attempt The Crystals' "Da Doo Ron Ron" at your own risk.

3. Make sure the text fits.

It's amazing how little text you can get on one side of a sweater, so this isn't going to work if you use big needles and chunky yarn. I use 3.25mm (US size 3) needles for the body, and 2.75mm (US size 2) for the rib. This works well with 4-ply yarn. Find a basic 4-ply sweater pattern you like (I use one from McGregor's book) and see how many stitches and rows you've got to play with. In this sweater, I used 2-ply "jumper weight" Shetland wool (which knits as 4-ply) from Jamieson & Smith, shetlandwool.org.

4. Create a design around the lyrics.

There's no substitute for inspiration and creativity here, and an appropriate design depends hugely on the song you've chosen. It helps if it has a clear theme. "1952 Vincent Black Lightning" has strong imagery, which inspired the gravestone design on the back. For simplicity (and readability), I suggest keeping the other design elements away from the lyrics. Also, don't forget the sleeves: adding or echoing part of the design here can be really effective. Use the spreadsheet to block out the design around the lyrics.

5. Sort out the spacing.

Getting the spacing right is fiddly but important. You just need 1 clear background stitch between each letter within a word. To separate words on the same line, use at least 3 background stitches. Adjusting the spacing to justify the text (align left-hand and right edges) is easy and looks really good. For vertical spacing between rows you need at least 1 background row, but more looks better. You also need to be careful to leave enough rows to separate the tallest letters (in this typeface all the uppercase letters and lowercase ones such as 'h', 'l', and 't' are 7 rows high) from the lowest ones on the row above (letters such as 'g', 'p', and 'y' descend 3 rows below the others).

6. Choose your colors.

I normally use plain colors when I'm working with text. You need to be careful to maintain a decent contrast between the text and the background. If you use a variegated yarn, then the color variation needs to be quite subtle to make sure the text stays readable. In the sweater designed around Tom Waits' "Dirt in the Ground" (Figure C), the text and the

surrounding chain design use a variegated yarn from 21st Century Yarns (21stcenturyyarns.com).

7. Start knitting.

In terms of technique there's nothing much to know: it's straightforward, plain knitting using a Fair Isle technique with a stockinette stitch (apart from the rib). Unlike conventional Fair Isle designs, you aren't repeating each color regularly, which means that you've potentially got some rather long floats of the text color yarn on the reverse. I try to catch them with the background color yarn every 5 stitches on average, and I try not to leave one longer than 7 stitches if I can avoid it.

8. Keep knitting.

Adding borders like the one shown in Figure C introduces a third color, but it's well away from the text so it doesn't really interfere — you might just need to untwist the different balls of yarn occasionally. I usually knit the sleeves, cuffs, and neck in the round, using double-ended needles to avoid having a seam, but you don't have to. This technique isn't recommended for the main body of the sweater, as it will give a lot of extra stranding at the sides.

9. Concentrate.

This isn't a project where you can knit on autopilot while doing 3 other things at the same time; every row is different, so take your time and check regularly for mistakes. It's difficult to say how long the whole sweater will take. Most of mine take 4 or 5 months, but I'm pretty slow and only knit in the evenings.

10. Stand still.

As with any slogan-bearing shirt, you need to be prepared to stop and stand still while people read what you're wearing. Do you want the words on the front or the back? In other words, do you prefer to have someone staring at your chest, or someone you can't see telling you not to turn around?

It's really satisfying to create a unique garment with connections to a song that you really love. There are a lot of songs out there … what are you waiting for?

Theo Wright is a technology manager by day and a knitter and handweaver by night. See flickr.com/photos/theowright for more photos or contact Theo at knit1.weave1@yahoo.co.uk.

Solar Jewelry

Fashion a luminous wrist cuff powered by solar jewels. BY ALICE PLANAS AND HATTI LIM

Photography by Hatti Lim; illustrations by Alice Planas

T he discovery of the photovoltaic effect (converting light energy to electricity at the atomic level) dates back to 1839, but for much of its history, solar energy as a readily available resource remained an elusive quest. In the 1950s, when developments in new materials (silicon) achieved major gains in efficiency, solar energy transitioned from a curious novelty to a promising possibility. These days, solar cells are developing rapidly, becoming lighter, smaller, clearer, and more flexible.

For a micro-scale project like jewelry, solar energy seems to be the perfect fit. Since these little gems require extended exposure to light in order to drive a momentary glow, we began to wonder — what's more precious than energy? In this project we invite crafters to discover solar energy as a material for jewelry.

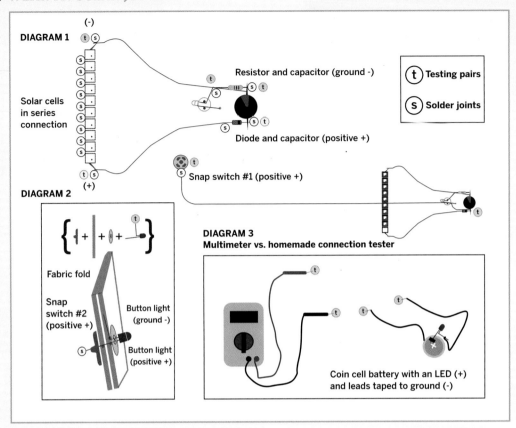

DIAGRAM 1

(-)

Solar cells in series connection

Resistor and capacitor (ground -)

(t) **Testing pairs**

(s) **Solder joints**

Diode and capacitor (positive +)

(+)

DIAGRAM 2

Snap switch #1 (positive +)

{ ⊣ + | + ⊗ + ⊣ }

Fabric fold

Snap switch #2 (positive +)

Button light (ground -)

Button light (positive +)

DIAGRAM 3
Multimeter vs. homemade connection tester

Coin cell battery with an LED (+) and leads taped to ground (-)

Materials

- » **Capacitor, 0.22 farad, 5.5V** Mouser Electronics part #555-DX5R5H224
- » **Solar cells, 0.5V, 1.9mA (10)** Mouser #782-BPW34
- » **Resistor, 1 kilohm** Mouser #660-CFS1/4CT52R102J
- » **Schottky diode, 30V, 1A** Mouser #512-1N5818
- » **3mm super bright LED** Mouser #638-1224UYCS5302
- » **Soldering iron and solder** RadioShack kit, part #64-2802
- » **Multimeter** RadioShack #22-810
- » **Wrapping wire** RadioShack #278-502
- » **Fabric (3"×11") and fabric shears**
- » **Sewing needle, pins, and thread**
- » **Metal snaps (2) and a button**
- » **Wire stripper, wire snips, and pliers**
- » **Small scissors**
- » **Nail polish, tape, ruler, and Sharpie**

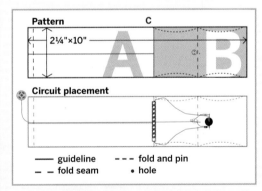

Pattern

C

2¼"×10"

A   B

Circuit placement

—— guideline   - - - fold and pin
– – fold seam   • hole

1. Make the wrist cuff.

a. Cut and mark the basic pattern for the wrist cuff (see above). Print the pattern at craftzine.com/06/wear_solar. The body of the cuff (Section A) measures 5¾" (¼" seam). Leave 4¼" (Section B) for containing the electronic circuit. We use wool felt because it holds its shape beautifully and doesn't fray.

b. Design a shape to cut from section A for an artful closure. Think of a simple repeating shape that forms an interesting texture. Practice on paper first. Draw

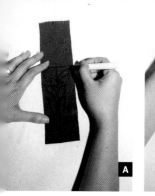

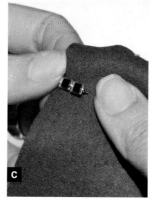

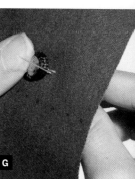

Fig. A: Plan your design, thinking about positive and negative shapes. Fig. B: A small sharp pair of scissors makes cutting easier. Fig. C: When piercing, make sure to touch the legs of the solar cells. Fig. D: Pushing the legs flat together makes for a secure connection. Fig. E: A line is easy to begin with. Fig. F: Bend the legs as close to the base as possible. Fig. G: Double check the diagram to make sure the capacitor is correctly oriented.

your pattern on section A (Figure A). Use small scissors to cut the shapes (Figure B).

2. Build the solar circuit.

a. Carefully study Diagram 1, also available at craftzine.com/06/wear_solar, paying attention to the components and connections.

b. Connect the solar cells together in a series as shown in Diagram 1. Following line C on the pattern, pierce the legs of each cell through the felt. Each cell has a positive leg (+) marked by a small dot, and a ground (-). Connect each cell's leg to the following cell's leg of the opposite value (Figure C) on the back side of the felt. Use pliers to bend the touching legs together flush against the felt (Figure D). Each cell delivers 0.5 volts — which alone is not enough to power the LED. Connected in series, all 10 cells combine to produce just under 5 volts (Figure E).

c. Bend the legs of the capacitor flat (Figure F). Match the ground (marked with a stripe) and positive leads of the capacitor with the solar cells. Sew the capacitor into the fabric (Figure G). The capacitor stores the charge from the cells. Be sure to match

ground to ground – this type of capacitor can blow up if connected backward.

d. Connect the 1N5818 diode to the capacitor's positive leg, and connect the resistor to its ground leg. The diode keeps the charge from leaking out of the capacitor; pay attention to the direction of the diode by looking for the stripe (Diagram 1). Use pliers to carefully twist the component legs around the capacitor leads. Snip off any excess wire.

e. Finish the circuit by connecting the components with wire, following the circuit placement diagram. Prepare each piece of wire by stripping off ½" from the ends with wire strippers (Figure H).

f. Cut a piece of wire that runs the length of the fabric. Attach one end to the positive leg of the capacitor, in front of the diode. The other end will connect to the female snap switch (Step 4).

g. Find the LED's positive and ground legs (see Diagram 2); usually the longer leg is positive, but you can test with a watch battery to be sure (Diagram 3). Pass the legs through the button from the outside of

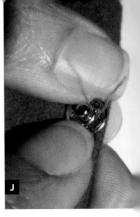

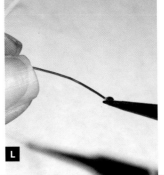
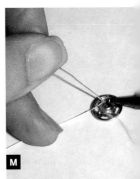

Fig. H: Make sure your wire stripper has a small enough setting for wrap wire. Fig. I: Pass the LED legs through the button from the outside. Fig. J: Larger buttons make the snap more secure when opening/closing.

Fig. K: Voltage should be registering from the cells, close to 5V under direct light. Fig. L: If your tip doesn't melt the solder easily, either it needs cleaning or it's not quite hot enough. Fig. M: Heating the joint for a strong solder.

the cuff (Figure I). Twist the ground leg of the LED to the other leg of the resistor (Diagram 1). Pierce the positive leg back through to the other side of the fabric (Figure J). This will connect to the male snap switch (Step 4).

3. Test, charge, and solder.
a. Test your circuit for mistakes and loose connections before soldering, using a multimeter. If you don't have a multimeter, a homemade testing device can be fashioned from a coin cell battery, an LED, tape, and wire (Diagram 3).

The multimeter is a tool that checks electrical connections and displays the electrical properties of a circuit. Its "continuity" feature indicates when 2 points are electrically connected (sometimes with a beep). Check for continuity by touching the 2 probes to each of the pairs marked on the diagrams with a T (Diagrams 1, 2, and 3).

b. Once you've checked the connections, leave the cuff under a lamp with the solar cells exposed to charge for 30 minutes. Then test the charge by reading the voltage from both legs of the capacitor with a multimeter (Figure K), or by simply

placing an LED across the capacitor to see if it will light.

c. Follow Diagram 1 and solder each of the points marked with an S.

❋ **TIPS: Use sandpaper to clean any residue from the tip of a cool soldering iron. Heat your iron, then "tin" it by touching solder to the tip of the hot iron and coating it (Figure L). Always solder joints in direct physical contact (twist or crimp the joints to eliminate gaps). A strong solder is achieved by heating the joint until solder melts to it when touched (Figure M). Use tape or glue to hold together tiny parts. Also, make sure to protect your furniture from the heat, and work in a ventilated area. For a short video tutorial on soldering, see craftzine.com/go/solder.**

4. Make a snap switch.
a. Take the metal snaps and separate the 2 sides. Solder the female side to the long wire that connects to the capacitor (Figure N). Solder the male side to the LED leg that protrudes from the fabric (Figure O).

Fig. N: Solder the wire to the bottom of the snap to keep it from being exposed. Fig. O: Twist the LED leg around the snap. Fig. P: Take time to make your stitches neat. Fig. Q: Make sure to leave room between the 2 snaps.

Fig. R: Search for beautiful elements to enhance your design. Fig. S: Be careful with your stitches and placement of elements. Fig. T: Calculate how long you need to expose your cuff to sunlight to charge.

b. Sew the snaps into place, reinforcing them by doubling up on the thread and stitches.

5. Insulate, sew, and finish.

a. Coat all exposed wires and soldered joints with clear nail polish. Set aside to dry.

b. Fold over the fabric on section B to cover the circuit. Fold under and pin the sides. Sew up the flap (Figure P).

c. Measure the cuff around your wrist and sew on a second snap (Figure Q). Add details such as decorative stitches and embellishments to enhance your design (Figures R and S).

Ready to Wear

The cuff is ready to shine (Figure T)! While charging, disconnect the snap switch. Use the second snap to fasten the cuff to your wrist. At night, snap the switch and enjoy the glow of energy collected over time (the light will last approximately 10 minutes).

Alice Planas and Hatti Lim love the idea of sustainable wearable electricity. Their solar jewelry (developed with Leif Krinkle and Meredith Silverman) can be seen at solarstarlights.com.

Resources

Electronic components for the solar circuit can be found at: mouser.com and solarbotics.com

Basic soldering supplies and tools: radioshack.com

Electronic Crafts by Mouna Andraos: electroniccrafts.org

Tech DIY by Ji Sun Lee has simple projects for moms and kids: techdiy.org

Leah Buechley's site is full of resources and inspiration for wearable technology: cs.colorado.edu/~buechley

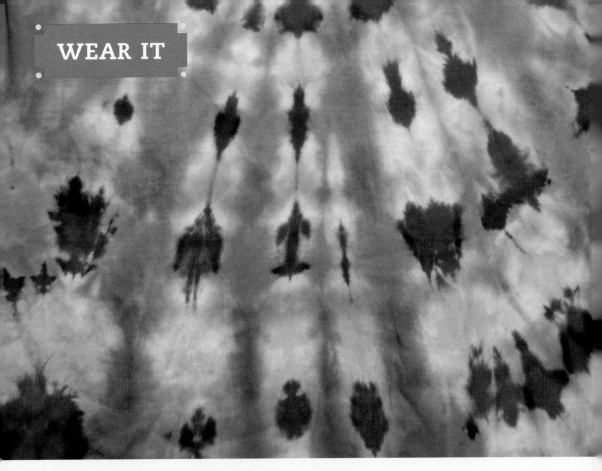

Tie-Dye Topology

Learn how to plan your spirals and swirls when dyeing your favorite Ts. BY EDWIN WISE

T ie-dye, glorious tie-dye! The bright swirl of colors can lighten the drabbest day. But when you start to make your own patterns, questions emerge. This project explores what really happens inside a tie-dyed spiral.

I lived in Oregon for 20 years and Austin, Texas, for another handful before I ever owned any tie-dye. The only reason I succumbed was because I made my own; there's a wonderful satisfaction in wearing something you created with your own hands.

After making many shirts in many patterns, the question arose amongst our little group of how to better control the pattern. Here I'll show you how to make classic spiral and radial patterns, illustrating the tie-dye process while unraveling the twisted topology involved.

Photography by Edwin Wise

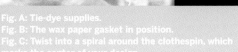

Fig. A: Tie-dye supplies.
Fig. B: The wax paper gasket in position.
Fig. C: Twist into a spiral around the clothespin, which marks the center of your design.

Fig. D: Hold the bundled T-shirt together firmly with rubber bands.

Materials

- » **Cotton T-shirts** The more the merrier. You can dye any cotton item: sheets, towels, pants, whatever.
- » **Procion fiber-reactive dye, powdered** 2–8tsp per 8oz of water
- » **Soda ash** 8oz per gallon of water
- » **Dye-carrying detergent** such as Synthrapol or Dharma's new nontoxic alternative
- » **Warm water**
- » **5gal bucket**
- » **Plastic squeeze bottles** 1 per color
- » **Waterproof gloves** rubber or vinyl
- » **Dust mask** to keep your lungs clean
- » **Rubber bands** or string
- » **Clothespins**
- » **Paper towels**
- » **Wax paper (optional)** for gaskets

1. Good Day Sunshine

While wearing clothes you don't love, put 3–4gal of hot water into your bucket and mix in 8oz soda ash per gallon. Following the manufacturer's instructions (and wearing a dust mask), mix up several colors of Procion fiber-reactive dye and pour into squeeze bottles. Soda ash may irritate your skin, and the dye will make your fingers interesting colors, so wear gloves now and throughout the entire process.

2. Fixing a Hole

To keep your bottles from leaking, seal them with wax paper. Cut 2" squares of paper, fold them in quarters, and cut off the corner that's made up of all inside-folds. Unfolded, you have a hole in the square! Put it over the bottle and fasten the lid over it (Figure B).

3. Twist and Shout

The essence of tie-dye is the *tying*; and it's not just tying, but rumpling, folding, pulling, and twisting the fabric and binding it into position. The ties can be loose, to hold the fabric in shape, or tight, changing the way dye infiltrates the fabric. This chaotic treatment makes sometimes unpredictable, and usually very interesting, patterns. Tie-dye is just one form of

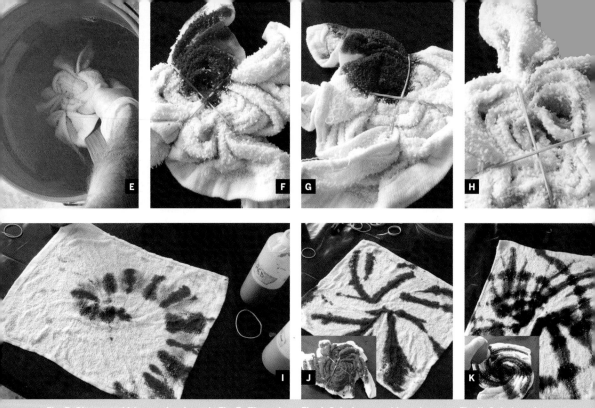

Fig. E: Give your shirt a good soda soak. Fig. F: The red quadrant (top) ... Fig. G: ... plus the blue quadrant (bottom) ... Fig. H: ... plus the yellow quadrant (middle) ... Fig. I: ... make a spiral!

Fig. J: Coloring one side makes rays. Fig. K: Spirals and lines untwist to lines and spirals — the dye lines produce the opposite pattern.

the ancient Japanese art of shibori, and the spiral pattern explored here is just one shape within tie-dye.

Find a clean, flat surface. To preserve your surface's finish, lay 2 layers of plastic over it (2 layers are *much* safer than 1). Lay a T-shirt out flat and clip a clothespin where you want the center of your pattern. Clip through both layers of fabric! Twist the shirt around the clothespin into a bundle (Figure C), taking care to tidy up its edges. Loop rubber bands, or tie cotton string, around the spiraled bundle to hold it together (Figure D).

4. Let It Be

Put the tied garment into the bucket of hot soda-ash water (Figure E). Poke and squeeze the air out, so it sinks. Leave it to soak for at least 5 minutes. This soak changes the chemistry of the fabric, raising its pH to about 10.5, which helps the Procion dye bond tightly to it. Also, wet fabric absorbs dye differently than dry fabric, softening the edges of the pattern.

5. Revolution

While your shirt is soaking, let's look closer at the pattern we're about to make. Since we twisted the shirt into a spiral, a *straight* line of dye applied

across the bundle should unwind into a spiral pattern.

As an example, we'll dye one wedge of a twisted washcloth. There are 3 areas where we can insert dye: the top (red, Figure F), the bottom (blue, Figure G), and the interior of the folds (yellow, Figure H).

Dye squirted onto the surface of the bundle will not spread very deep into the folds, so you have to push dye into the folds with the tip of the bottle. Laid flat, you can see the resulting spiral of color: red-yellow-blue-yellow-red, spiraling out from the center (Figure I).

6. Here Comes the Sun

If dyeing one wedge creates a spiral, does dyeing the entire surface create more spirals? Nope — dyeing and unfolding just one side of a test cloth creates ... rays of color radiating out from the center (Figure J). Interesting!

7. Sun King

If straight dye lines make spiral patterns, what do spiraling dye lines make? They create straight patterns! If you dye the edge of some cloth spirals (blue), they unwind into straight(ish) lines, depending on how careful you were. Straight lines (red) spin out into 4 spirals as expected (Figure K).

L M

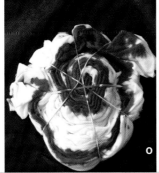

N O

P

Fig. L: Alternating red and yellow on the front.
Fig. M: Alternating green and blue on the back. This combo creates the pattern shown on page 128.

Fig. N: Four quadrants of blue ... Fig. O: ... plus spirals of red ... Fig. P: ... make blue spirals and red rays.

8. All Together Now

It's time to dye some shirts. Be sure to get the color deep into the folds, especially if you don't like white in your tie-dye. Note that some colors mix together in a pretty manner (red plus blue gives purple, etc.), while other colors mix into ... mud.

Keep your surface clean! You need to use a lot of dye, and it drips. When finished, wrap each shirt in a plastic bag and let it set undisturbed for 24 hours.

After 24 hours, rinse the bundled shirts in water, unbundle them, and continue rinsing until the water runs mostly clear. Immediately machine-wash the shirts with a textile detergent, such as Synthrapol, which helps carry the excess dye away. Now the shirts should be colorfast and stay bright for years.

9. Helter Skelter

This shirt pictured on page 128 was dyed with 4 colors; red and yellow alternating on the top (Figure L), and green and blue alternating on the bottom (Figure M). The colors were pushed down into the folds so they met in the middle, but with minimal overlap. The result is a bright, cheery shirt with a simple spiral. The extra-bright red dye stands out in the pattern and creates a radial effect.

10. The Long and Winding Road

While some tie-dye practitioners abhor white (some go so far as to start with pre-colored shirts), I don't mind white. I use white in this example as a backdrop for a pattern of blue spirals and red lines, each dyed onto their own side of the twisted bundle (Figures N, O, and P).

Resources

My supplies and most of my technical data are from Dharma Trading Company: dharmatrading.com

➕ More of my tie-dye shirts can be seen at simreal.com/tiedye.html.

Many thanks to Matt and Susan Pinsonneault for teaching me to tie and dye in the first place and for the use of their garage and colors for this project, to Marla Wise who provided extra hands where needed, and to Dharma Trading for being awesome.

Edwin Wise is a software engineer and rogue technologist, developing software during the day and exploring the edges of mad science at night.

EMBROIDERY

By Dolin O'Shea

Learn to paint pictures with floss and fabric.

Gussy up some fabric with easy decorative stitches that will wow your friends and family. To embroider basically means to decorate material with needlework. Embroidery is based on hand-sewing stitches, and encompasses many different forms of stitching: cross-stitch, crewel, quilting, needlepoint, and much more.

What you'll be learning here is good ol' basic embroidery, the type that Jenny Hart of Sublime Stitching has made so hip and cool. Once you know the basics, try experimenting with different types of threads, stitches, and fabrics. I think of embroidering like painting — your floss is the paint and your fabric is the canvas. You can illustrate many beautiful things with just a few stitches under your belt.

Photography by Natalie Zee Drieu

»

BASICS »

Embroidery is very easy. All you need is a needle, floss, an embroidery hoop, your imagination, and some material. It's also very portable, so you can do it during your commute, hanging out with your friends, or in front of the TV. If you're just starting out, your design should be a simple line drawing, or you can use a heat-transferred embroidery design, available for purchase. Gather up all the necessary materials, sit down, get cozy, and start your stitching!

START »

1. PREP YOUR FABRIC

1a. Pre-wash the fabric before you start — that way you won't have to deal with the fabric shrinking and puckering after you've done all your fancy needlework.

1b. Cut your fabric. Your fabric needs to be at least a few inches larger on all sides than the embroidery design, so that you can easily put the embroidery hoop on your fabric. If you're using a tea towel or an item of clothing, make sure you place your design far enough from the edge so that you can isolate that fabric on the embroidery hoop.

1c. Transfer your design to your fabric. For the seahorse design, I taped the design with the fabric over it to a bright sunny window, then traced over it with a water-soluble fabric pen. If you're transferring your design onto darker fabric, you'll need to get some carbon transfer paper in a light color to trace onto your fabric.

2. PUT YOUR FABRIC IN THE HOOP

Place the inner embroidery hoop on a flat surface, lay your fabric over the hoop with your design centered, then place the outer hoop over both inner hoop and fabric. You may need to gently pull the edges of the fabric, after getting the hoop on, to make the fabric taut, like a drum.

MATERIALS

» YOUR DESIGN
» A WAY TO TRANSFER YOUR DESIGN TO FABRIC. THIS CAN BE A WATER-SOLUBLE FABRIC PEN, HEAT TRANSFER PENCIL, OR A PURCHASED HEAT-TRANSFERRED DESIGN.
» EMBROIDERY HOOP. A GOOD BASIC SIZE TO START WITH WOULD BE A 7" HOOP.
» EMBROIDERY NEEDLES (LIKE BASIC HAND-SEWING NEEDLES BUT WITH A LARGER EYE)
» 100% COTTON PLAIN WEAVE FABRIC IN A LIGHT COLOR, SUCH AS A TEA TOWEL, MUSLIN, OR POPLIN
» SMALL SHARP SCISSORS
» FABRIC SCISSORS (OPTIONAL), NOT NECESSARY IF YOU'RE EMBROIDERING A FINISHED OBJECT, LIKE A TEA TOWEL, HANKY, OR ITEM OF CLOTHING
» 6-STRAND COTTON EMBROIDERY FLOSS

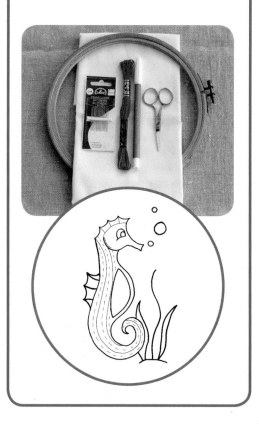

3. START YOUR STITCHIN'

3a. Cut your floss in lengths 12"–15". Any longer than that and your stitching arm will get tired from all the pulling and reaching. You'll also run into more of the dreaded tangling factor with longer pieces of floss.

3b. Thread your needle. You may want to moisten the end of the floss a bit with your mouth, to help keep all the strands together. Pull about 3"–4" through the eye of the needle; this gives you something to grip onto, so your needle doesn't come unthreaded. Then knot the other end of the floss.

   Some embroidery purists insist on not using any knots when starting and stopping their stitches — they think it can look sloppy and cause excess bulkiness on the back of their work. I say knot away in the beginning, and then if you want to go the purist route later when you're a pro stitcher, you can.

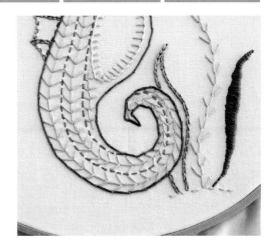

3c. Go over your design with the stitches of your choice (see the list of stitches, below), making sure to cover as much of the traced lines as possible. If you're using a heat-transferred pattern, this is really important, as the ink doesn't always wash out.

4. CLEAN UP

Once you've finished stitching your design, some of your pen marks may still show. You can spray your fabric lightly with water (while it's still in the hoop) and those water-soluble pen marks will disappear. Let it dry in the hoop. Once dry, remove your work from the hoop and press with an iron on a terry cloth towel, with your design facedown on the towel. You don't want to flatten all your fancy stitching. That's it — so easy!

STITCHES

NOTE: The colors of the stitches on the finished seahorse embroidery correspond with the tutorial images, except for the split stitch.

1. Running stitch (*medium coral*)
One of the most basic stitches, it's used a lot in hand-sewing. Pull your needle over and under the fabric at regular intervals.

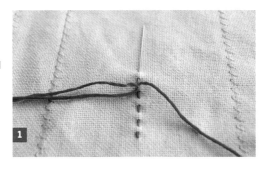

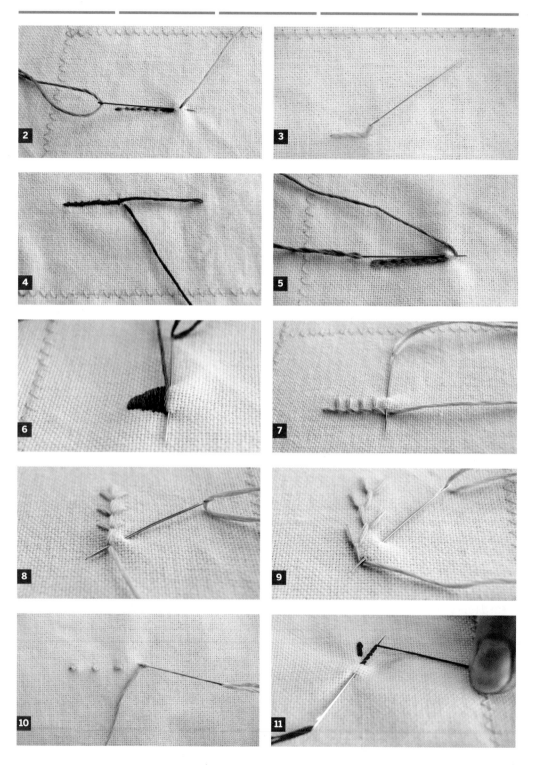

STITCHES CONTINUED

2. Back stitch (*medium turquoise*)
Another basic stitch you may have learned in hand-sewing. Pull your needle up through the fabric, make a stitch backward, and then bring your needle back up through the fabric in front of the stitch you just made. Continue the backward-and-forward stitching.

3. Split stitch (*dark brown on seahorse, light turquoise in tutorial*) Make a single stitch, then pull your needle up through the middle of the stitch you just made, splitting the strands of the floss.

4. Couching (*dark turquoise and dark coral*)
Place your floss flat along the fabric, then thread a second piece of floss and make small stitches over the floss that's flat along the fabric.

5. Chain stitch (*medium green*)
Pull your needle up through the fabric, insert it in almost the same place you just pulled it through, making sure to leave a small loop, then bring your needle back up through the inside of the loop you just made.

6. Satin stitch (*dark green*)
This stitch is a series of straight stitches filling in a small area. Stitches are made very close to each other, creating a smooth, filled-in surface.

7. Blanket stitch (*peach*)
Work this stitch from left to right. Pull your needle up through the fabric, then insert it back down at a point above and to the right of where you just brought it up. Bring your needle back up through the fabric a short distance to the right of the first stitch, making sure the floss loop is caught under your needle.

8. Fern stitch (*light turquoise*)
Make 3 stitches at a slight angle to each other, all starting out of the same hole, and then continue these 3 stitches downward.

9. Feather stitch (*light green*)
Pull your needle up through the fabric, then insert it a little to the right, creating a small loop. Bring it back up again a little below the 2 points, making sure to keep the floss loop under the needle. Then repeat the same stitches a little to the left. Continue the left-to-right motion, working this stitch downward.

10. French knot (*light gray*)
Pull your needle up through the fabric, wrap the floss around the needle a couple of times (hold the wrapped floss loops close to the fabric) and insert the needle a very short distance away.

11. Bullion stitch (*dark coral*)
Insert your needle, then pull just the needle's point up through the fabric a short distance away (this distance will be the length of your bullion stitch). Wrap your floss around the needle's point at least 6 times, holding the wrapped floss close to the fabric. Pull the needle up all the way through, and reinsert it back down where you first pulled it through the fabric.

FINISH ☒

RESOURCES

Mary Thomas' *Dictionary of Embroidery Stitches*, revised by Jan Eaton, Trafalgar Square Publishing, 1998

The Art of Embroidery by Francoise Tellier-Loumange, Thames & Hudson, 2007

Sublime Stitching sublimestitching.com
For all your basic embroidery needs and how-tos.

Michaels michaels.com
This arts and crafts supply chain has everything you need to get started, except fabric.

Dolin O'Shea has worked in the fashion industry as a technical designer and pattern maker for the last 15 years. She loves all crafty things having to do with needles, thread, fabric, and yarn. Find her at lulubliss.typepad.com.

PARTY PIÑATA

Create a festive, personalized piñata that's easy to make and fun to break.

By Brian Anderson

- » **Balloons**
- » **Newspaper**
- » **Masking tape**
- » **Flour and water**
- » **Mixing bowl**
- » **Whisk**
- » **Empty cardboard tubes** from paper towels and toilet paper
- » **White glue**
- » **Crepe paper**
- » **Scissors**
- » **Cardboard**
- » **Wire hanger**
- » **Long-nose pliers**

P iñatas add great excitement to any party. But instead of settling for a store-bought design (often made of child-proof cardboard), consider making your own custom piñata. Piñata-making is part art and part engineering, so it's fun for the whole brain. Best of all, the decorating process hides all your mistakes.

This example shows the construction of a spider piñata, but the same techniques can be used to create any sort of piñata you choose. The materials are inexpensive, and the process is challenging, fun, and easy. So take a whack at making your own piñata, and it won't be long before everyone else is taking a whack at it, too!

Brian Anderson has been making custom piñatas in Austin, Texas, since 1995. He is also the author of the book series *The Adventures of Commander Zack Proton* (Simon & Schuster).

1. SHAPE THE SPIDER'S BODY

The spider's abdomen is made from a 12" party balloon. The front section of its body (the prosoma) is flat and nearly round on the sides. This shape is made by bending 2 long balloons into spirals and taping them together (Figure A).

2. WRAP THE BODY SECTIONS

Wrap the balloons in a layer of newspaper, and tape it all down using masking tape. Cut off any excess newspaper to help smooth out the shapes.

3. MAKE THE PAPIER-MÂCHÉ PASTE

Using the mixing bowl and whisk, mix up equal amounts of flour and water (for example, 1 cup of flour and 1 cup of water) to form a paste.

4. PAPIER-MÂCHÉ THE BODY SECTIONS

Tear newspaper into 1"-wide strips, and dip them one at a time into the paste. Squeegee off excess paste by running the strips between 2 fingers, then lay the strips onto the newspaper-wrapped balloons. Once a balloon is covered in a layer of strips, let it dry, then apply 2 or 3 more layers of papier-mâché, allowing each one to dry in between.

5. ATTACH THE BODY SECTIONS

Attach the 2 body sections of the spider with masking tape (Figure B), then lay a couple of layers of papier-mâché strips across the joint to

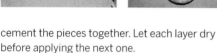

cement the pieces together. Let each layer dry before applying the next one.

6. CREATE THE LEGS

The legs are made from empty paper towel and toilet paper tubes (Figure C). Attach the leg segments using masking tape, then wrap a few layers of papier-mâché strips around them to give them strength. In these photos, the front of the spider's body had to be propped up until the legs had enough strength to support its weight (Figure D).

7. POP THE BALLOONS

Once the papier-mâché sculpture is finished, cut a small hole in each balloon section to pop the balloons and remove them. Cover the small holes with papier-mâché or even some masking tape.

8. ADD THE HOOK

Adding the hook is one of the most important parts of making a piñata, because the hook has to bear the weight of the filled piñata. First cut a piece of hanger wire or other stiff wire and, using long-nose pliers, bend it around a small piece of cardboard. Cut the piñata open somewhere on its side and insert the cardboard and wire. Then punch the wire through the top and center of the piñata from the inside.

Once the wire is sticking out the top, bend it into a hook using pliers. Then close up the hole on the side of the piñata using papier-mâché, or masking tape, since you'll cover it with decoration anyway.

NOTE: When inserting the cardboard and wire, make sure it's from the side and not the top of the piñata, as you don't want to weaken the area from which the piñata will be hanging.

9. PAINT THE PIÑATA (OPTIONAL)

I spray-painted this piñata before decorating it, to get an idea of how the colors would look when fully decorated, but this step isn't necessary.

10. WEAKEN A THICK WALL

If your piñata wall seems too thick, weaken it by stabbing it repeatedly with a small knife.

11. DECORATE!

Use your imagination when decorating! I usually use crepe paper instead of paint because it hides any flaws, and looks festive when it's fluffed up. Cut ¼"-wide fringe into a crepe paper streamer, then use white glue to attach the crepe paper to the piñata. I wanted to create a variety of textures on the spider piñata, so I used snipped crepe paper on the legs with finer snips at the joints (Figure E), and unsnipped crepe paper on the shell-like prosoma. To create the "hairy" abdomen on the spider, I applied spray-on adhesive and then pressed on loose handfuls of shredded, black gift-bag tissue paper.

12. FILL THE PIÑATA

Use scissors or a small knife to cut a small door in the top of the piñata for filling. Fill the piñata with candy and toys. Fold the door back down and it will usually be hard to spot.

13. TAKE A SWING AT IT

Party time! Hang the piñata and let the whacking commence!

➕ For more piñata-making tips and examples, visit my website pinataboy.com.

Photography by Brian Anderson

Bleach Shirt Stencil

You want a design on a T-shirt and you want it *now*! Sometimes the best designs come out of desperation. Here's how to put a cool design on a T-shirt ASAP!

You will need: Dark T-shirt, gloves, safety goggles, bleach, spray bottle, piece of cardboard, pen or pencil, marker, paper, scissors, sink, water, spray-adhesive tack (optional)

1. Prepare.

Put on gloves and safety goggles. Mix up a batch of 50/50 bleach to water solution in a spray bottle. Label it, and draw a skull and crossbones on the bottle so nobody mistakenly thinks it contains water. Then put a piece of cardboard inside the shirt so the bleach doesn't bleed through.

2. Design.

Draw a stencil design on paper and cut it out. Just remember that it's going to be a stencil, so it should be designed so it can be filled in with color (or bleach). Bleach can bleed into the shirt, so keep it simple and be bold. When you're done, place the design on the shirt. I put some spray-adhesive tack on the back of the stencil so it would stick to the shirt a bit.

3. Bleach.

Set your sprayer to a fine mist and spray the bleach solution over the stencil. Watch the color disappear before your eyes.

4. Rinse.

If you leave the bleach on too long, it'll make the fabric disintegrate, so when it's getting close to the right color, dunk the shirt in a sink full of water and rinse until it doesn't smell like bleach. Dry it out, and you're good to go — your T-shirt design is done!

Photography by Nora Abousteit

Bre Pettis produces podcasts for MAKE and CRAFT magazines. He shows how to make cool things at makezine.com/podcast.

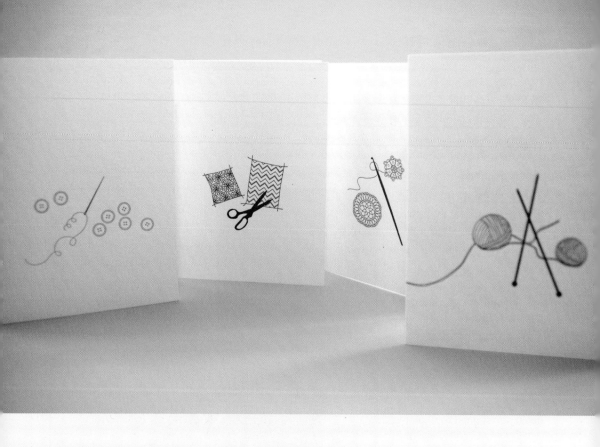

BAZAAR

CRAFTY GOODS WE ADORE. *Compiled by Natalie Zee Drieu*

Letterpress Card Set

$12

palindromepress.etsy.com

I swooned when I saw this wonderful homage to crafters everywhere. I'm a sucker for letterpress printing, and these cards, in simple black and white with luxurious paper and clean lines, immediately caught my eye. I bought the set of four (quilting squares, knitting needles with balls of yarn, crocheted snowflakes with a hook, and a needle and thread with buttons), sent one to a friend, and then greedily framed the other three to hang over my craft corner (aka overflowing closet).

—*Arwen O'Reilly*

Art School Dropout >> Zipper Pouch

$18
artschooldropout.net

The beautiful and sturdy vinyl zipper pouches by Jessee Maloney's Art School Dropout are a dream for any crafter. I love my Bird on a Branch pouch for its detailed appliqué embroidery and for its larger form factor. This bag fits all the tools I need for my craft projects when I'm on the go, from crochet hooks to small notebooks to those little bits and pieces that easily get lost in a tote bag. Choose from a variety of pouch sizes and designs such as cake and sweets, deer, and swallows.

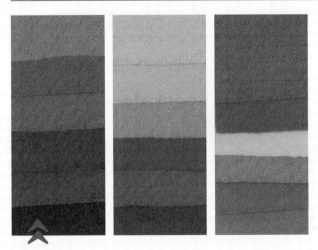

Mary Flanagan Hand-Dyed Felted Wool

$23
purlsoho.com

On a trip to New York City last fall, I visited Purl Patchwork in SoHo and had the wonderful experience of actually seeing the Mary Flanagan hand-dyed felted wool pieces in person. Once I touched the soft wool I couldn't help myself — I knew I had to get some. From the large selection of vibrant and muted colors, it was hard to pick just a few. If you can't make it to New York, shop online and choose from 3 different color sets: Blues, Party Mix (rainbow colors), and Wheat Field. Each set gives you 6 generous pieces of different colored felt.

Dahle Trim Ruler 13"

$20
artcity.com

When it comes to working with paper, I'm a stickler for cutting straight lines. But X-Acto knives are out when I need to craft with children. I found this Dahle Trim Ruler on a recent trip to the art store and it's my new favorite crafting tool. The ruler comes with an attached, recessed blade that's easy to push down to cut but is safe for your fingers and hands. The slim but long self-healing mat allows me to cut large pieces of paper. The trim ruler also comes with 2 extra blade inserts to create decorative wavy and perforated designs. The whole set is super light for easy portability.

« French General Bracelet Jewelry Kit

$24
frenchgeneral.com

Ooh la la! Make yourself a vintage-style charm bracelet with trinkets that look like they came from the Paris flea market. It comes with everything you need in a cute little tin — you just supply your own tools. Choose from a variety of charm themes and colors.

Cathy of California Pincushion Kit

$8
cathyofcalifornia.com

For a mere 8 bucks, not only do I have a stylish pincushion, but I had fun making it too. The kit comes with a styrofoam ball, a piece of vintage material from Cathy's personal collection (which makes each pincushion kit unique), some felt to create flower petals, a decorative bee and flower bud, and of course instructions. (Necessary scissors, pencil, and pins are not included.) Now that I've learned the secret to pincushion construction, I'm inspired to make more as gifts using different shapes and my own fabrics. —Carla Sinclair

ElectroPUFF Lamp Dimmer Kit

$28
ifmachines.com

A little bit mod, a little bit hilarious, these fuzzy lamp dimmers will astonish and delight anyone who walks through your door. Using conductive yarns, IFM has created a cuddly pompom that senses the electrical current in your body to control your lamps. If perfection is what you're after, you should probably shell out another $5 and buy the completed dimmer, but if you want to teach your kids (or yourself) a little more about "soft" electronics, the kit is a great way to go. It took about half an hour to put together, and after a little time in the dryer and some trimming, my pompom looked pretty darn good. I spent a good five minutes turning my bedside lamp on and off when I was done, just for the thrill of it.   AO'R

Dritz Gripper Plier Kit

$14
joann.com

When Moxie taught me how to needle-felt a wristband, she whipped out her Dritz Gripper Plier to fasten the snaps directly on the felt. I ended up getting one right away because it's a great crafty tool to help fasten anything from bags to baby clothes. The kit comes with plenty of large snaps as well as tiny eyelets, perfect to get you started.

≪ The DIY Wedding

By Kelly Bare Chronicle Books $15

chroniclebooks.com

I'm getting married this summer and this book is by far my favorite! It's practical, fun, and full of good advice for anyone who wants to skip out on a planner, save money, or just make their wedding less like everybody else's. Each chapter has a few quick DIY how-tos and many helpful tips about contracts, vendors, and making the most of your friends and family. Bare helps you allocate your resources, whether it's time, money, or energy. It's a scary world out there in wedding land, but it doesn't have to be! —AO'R

≪ Kyuuto! Japanese Crafts: Lacy Crochet

By Shufu-To-Seikatsu Sha Chronicle Books $15

chroniclebooks.com

After years of drooling over Japanese craft books, I can finally read them thanks to Chronicle Books' newly translated Japanese book series, *Kyuuto! Japanese Crafts: Lacy Crochet* stands out with projects for delicate crochet cozies, modern doilies, and bags. The book does a great job in keeping with the tradition of Japanese craft books, giving lots of room for pages of thumbnail step-by-step photos and illustrated charts to help you achieve each project.

≪ Photocraft: Cool Things to Do with the Pictures You Love

By Caroline Herter, Laurie Frankel, and Laura Lovett Bulfinch Press $20

hachettebookgroupusa.com

Photocraft: Cool Things to Do with the Pictures You Love brings together the photo, digital, and material worlds with very imaginative and personal results. Any beginner can find lots to do, and for the advanced photo image crafter, there are plenty of ideas that can easily germinate more advanced projects. Each project is so fresh and stylish that you'll feel compelled to make it. —Jenny Mountjoy

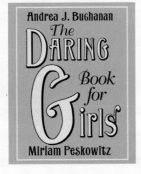

≪ The Daring Book for Girls

By Andrea J. Buchanan and Miriam Peskowitz Harper Collins $25

harpercollins.com

Reading *The Daring Book for Girls*, I am reminded of when I was a young Girl Scout. It's chock full of projects, facts, and fun bits that made me savor each page. I enjoyed thinking about far away islands and how I used to ace double-dutch jump rope on the playground. From making paper flowers to a lemon-powered clock, the projects cover a wide range of science, math, nature, and general crafts. It's the perfect all-in-one-book for girls and girls-at-heart to cozy up to.

Lee Meredith
Recycle It

» Lee Meredith, also known by the moniker Leethal, is a designer, photographer, and creator of things, living in Portland, Ore. She sells the things she makes from recycled materials, and shows you how to make them yourself in her DIY blog and zine (do stuff!), all found at leethal.net.

Vinyl Remix

Put a new spin on old records.

All thrift store shoppers are well aware of the massive piles of worthless vinyl records that gather dust on the shelves at every Goodwill, Salvation Army, and Savers in the country. Sure, some of us enjoy the hunt for that rare Beatles or Madonna album for $1 that might sell for 20 times that at a used record store, but most modern crafters would rather listen to their iPods.

Poor unwanted vinyl, we can't let it all go to the landfill! So, crafty thrifters, next time you see that dusty stack, dig through it for the wackiest covers, coolest artwork, and kitschiest designs; there's plenty to be done with both the vinyl and the sleeves!

MELTED VINYL BOWLS

These are definitely the most common craft use for records, and they are popular for a reason. A great project for any level of craft experience, record bowls require nothing but a bowl and an oven, take very little time, and are ready to use right away. Of course, if you're lucky enough to come across any colored records, grab them and enjoy the beautiful results of melted colored vinyl (Figure A)!

1. Preheat the oven to 200° F and find an oven-safe bowl at least 10" in diameter. Grab some other bowls for shaping the vinyl — a few different sizes will add variety. While preheating, you can wash your old records like plates, and be sure to open a window for air circulation!

2. Flip the big bowl upside down, place a 12" vinyl LP record centered on top, and put it in the oven. Leave it for 3–5 minutes, depending on the thickness of the vinyl. You can always throw it back in if it's not pliable enough.

3. Once out, peel the record off (careful, it's hot!) and put it into the same bowl or a cool one (Figure B).

You'll have to act quickly before it hardens (in about 30 seconds), but you can shape it however you want. Simply pushing the record into a big bowl will create the classic wavy record bowl. You can also try pushing a second bowl into the hot vinyl from the top to flatten out the curves. Experiment with different-sized bowls and sandwiching methods to get new shapes.

You can also melt 45s, aka 7" records, using the same process but a bit less time in the oven; you'll have more limited shaping options.

Photography by Lee Meredith

MAIL SORTERS

Make your desktop more rockin' by using records to hold your paperwork. This project looks great with either LPs cut in half (Figure C) or whole 45s (Figure D). All you need is a basic sorter, either thrifted/recycled or found cheap at discount stores.

For the 7" version, just attach the records to the sorter using glue or 2-sided tape. The LP version takes a little more effort:

1. Use scissors or a craft blade and a straightedge to score where you want to break the record.

2. Go over the line many times until you have a deep groove. Repeat the groove on the reverse side.

3. Carefully break the record — if it doesn't break after some effort, make your grooves deeper. Break as many records as you need for your sorter — either all half-records, or varying heights.

4. Glue or tape records to sorter.

You can also do this same project with only 2 records or 2 halves for a napkin holder.

CLOCKS

This project uses both the vinyl and the album covers. While you're vinyl hunting at the thrift store, stop by the clock section and grab one with good-looking working hands that looks easy to disassemble.

1. To make your new rock-clock, pop the top off, pull off the hands, and detach the battery-holding clock mechanism from the back.

2. For a vinyl clock (Figure E), stick the clock mechanism through the record hole — you might need to make the hole a little bigger by twisting a scissor blade in it to shave off a few layers. Then tape or glue it to the record, and push the hands back on the front.

3. For a cover art clock (Figure F), poke/punch a hole in the center of the sleeve, attach the clock mechanism on the back, and replace the hands. You can paint, stamp, or decoupage numbers on it if you want.

CD/DVD CASES

Sure, CDs are so 20th century, but those of us who use tons of CD-Rs to back up JPEGs, or have collections of DVD-R videos, need somewhere to store them. Besides, not *everyone* has an iPod! So turn that case for super-old media into a case for semi-old media (Figure I) — retro on so many levels.

You'll need: 1 album sleeve, six 2-sided CD pockets with holes on one edge (you can grab a big pack at an office supply store for a few dollars), and a strip of elastic or velcro. Pick up some thin frosted vinyl material (optional) if your case will endure a lot of use.

1. Cut your LP's front cover into a rectangle a little less than 12" long and about 5½" wide (or lay 2 CD pockets on top to determine how wide and long the case should be). Cut a rectangle a little smaller from the back cover — this will be the inside of your case.

2. Use a scissor blade to lightly score where you want the case to crease — on the front side of the cover piece, and the backside of the inner piece. You'll want 1"–1½" between the score lines, and less for the inner piece, so they fit together. Fold the pieces.

3. Cut 2 sections of vinyl about 1½" longer and wider than the 2 cover pieces — enough extra to wrap around all 4 sides and sew securely. Sew the vinyl around the LP cover pieces, making sure to stretch it tight (but not too tight!) as you go around. You're sewing through a layer of vinyl, the album cardboard, and a second layer of vinyl.

If you'll be machine sewing, before you begin with these materials, test what works best with your machine by using scraps of album cover and vinyl. Practice until you feel comfortable — it can be tricky.

4. Line up the 2 pieces to sew them together, first placing the elastic between them near the edge of the backside (Figure G). Sew the elastic into the case as you attach the pieces, but be very careful as it stretches across the second side — you don't want to sew it down where it shouldn't be sewn down. You'll have to break your thread to move past the elastic and continue. Go very slowly, as you're sewing through 2 layers of cardboard and 4 layers of vinyl.

5. You may prefer to use velcro flaps for the closure instead of elastic. Sew 2 squares onto the outside

corners of the case, and make 2 flaps with the vinyl material and the matching velcro squares to fold over and close the case.

6. Now your case just needs CD pockets. This part can be tough because the pockets are so slippery and difficult to work with. Line up the hole-punched edge strips so that half the pockets are on the left and half are on the right, then sew the pockets together (Figure H). Finally, sew the complete set into the case.

CUSTOM NOTEBOOKS

Use your favorite album artwork to make new covers for notebooks, journals, sketchbooks, photo albums, or any other book that needs to pop (Figure J). You can also add a strip of elastic to hold the notebook closed and carry other papers inside.

1. Grab any notebook with a cover thick enough to stay intact when the cardboard is glued on.

2. Cut 2 pieces of the record sleeve exactly the size of the front and back covers (Figure K). Think about how the covers will need to bend — score lines on the backs to help them bend if needed.
   Cut your elastic long enough to wrap all the way around the notebook once.

3. Glue the front cover on with a generous amount of white glue. Turn over to glue on the back cover, but first put the elastic in place. Wrap it around the front, see how it will close, and glue it down on the back of the notebook so the 2 ends meet in the middle. Glue the back cover on, using plenty of glue on both sides of the elastic.

4. Place the notebook on top of a hard book or floor, and bury it with many more hard, heavy books to press it flat. It's a good idea to layer album cover scraps or waste paper atop and beneath the notebook, so that the glue doesn't get on your books. Let press overnight, or for as long as the glue recommends.

MORE IDEAS

Cut your covers into postcard-sized pieces and mail notes to your friends. Or cut business-card-sized pieces, write your website/blog/email address on the back, and give them out as one-of-a-kind punk-rock business cards. Any project that uses cardboard pieces 12"×12" or smaller can be jazzed up by substituting album covers.

Use the LP bowls as gift baskets, or for food items — chips, popcorn, bread — with a napkin or plate underneath to keep crumbs from falling through the hole. That hole can act as built-in drainage for small plants (Figure L). The 7" bowls make great ashtrays, candle holders, or candy dishes. ✂

➕ There are even more fun projects online. Go to craftzine.com/go/ followed by the desired project name:

» Vinyl wall-mount mail holder: vinylmail
» Vinyl cuffs: vinylcuffs
» Vinyl coasters: vinylcoasters
» Album cover accordion scrapbook: albumscrap
» Album cover CD box: albumCDbox
» Album cover purse: albumpurse

Wendy Tremayne
Re: Fitted

» Wendy Tremayne (gaiatreehouse.com) is renovating an RV park into a 100% reuse off-grid B&B in Truth or Consequences, N.M. Another project, Swap-O-Rama-Rama (swaporamarama.org), is a clothing swap and DIY workshop designed to offer people an alternative to consumerism.

Under Rusted Stars

It's easy to imagine the heaps of camping gear lying about collecting dust in thrift shops across America, even as countless commuters in city subway cars and suburban SUVs emit thoughts of longing for the great outdoors: "I really am the outdoorsy type ..."

Like contact sports, camping lives in the collective consciousness as something that comes naturally. But Gaia's terrain is less predictable than the man-made environment that urban and suburban dwellers have grown accustomed to, and so, few are the folk who actually use a camping stove until the time of its natural expiration.

Something downright magical happens when the right gleaner and the right piece of junk — a match of near-perfect chemistry — find one another, and would-be trash is morphed into something new, something that seems even more right than what it was originally intended for. Andrew Martinez has whipped up many such alchemical pairings.

Most recently, Martinez found an old Coleman camping stove at Goodwill and modified it to fulfill his need for a bathroom cabinet. The cabinet he wanted to replace was too shallow, and ready-made choices were expensive, junky, and so standard in size that they couldn't fit the unique space. Five bucks and a vision of the old Coleman gutted, cleaned, and mounted to the wall just above the john repaid Martinez' patience.

Every forager has an eye for particular materials. Martinez likes metal objects. Old, new, rusted, and reconfigured metal things adorn a fence that he made to add privacy to the front yard of his home. The enclosure sports vintage car fenders, a rusty choo-choo train mobile, empty film reels, and abstract metal art pieces of his design. All are curiously mounted on, in, and around found wood and metal verticals that are seamlessly butted together.

As if to add a punch line to the wonderland of this enclosure, a naked chair stripped of its stuffing and re-planked with imaginatively shaped wood slats invites visitors to take a load off. What began as a shortage of options and led to a taste for reuse has resolved itself in a one-of-a-kind palate and good design. Martinez' idiosyncrasies now serve as a reminder to passersby that amongst the stale impression left by monotonous development, there still reside living beings engaged in authentic play.

Something downright magical happens when the right gleaner and the right piece of junk find one another.

Photograph by Andrew Martinez

DIY CAMPING STOVE CABINET

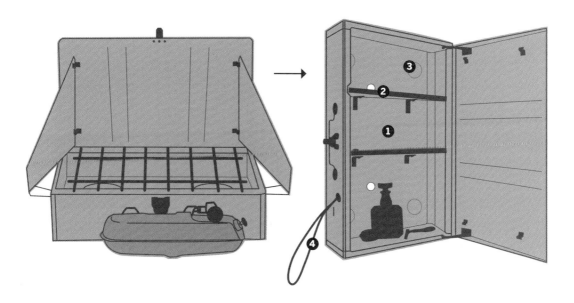

MATERIALS

- » MARKER/CRAYON
- » ¼" THICK MASONITE AKA HARD-BOARD, FOR SHELVES
- » CORNER BRACKETS (4) IDEALLY NO LESS THAN ½ THE DEPTH OF THE SHELF
- » SMALL BOLTS WITH NUTS (16) WASHERS OPTIONAL
- » DRYWALL ANCHORS WITH SCREWS (4) FOR MOUNTING TO WALL
- » POWER DRILL
- » SCREWDRIVER
- » SAW HAND, FRAMING, JIG, OR TABLE
- » LEVEL OR MEASURING TAPE
- » CRESCENT WRENCH TO GUT THE STOVE OF ITS PREVIOUS CONTENTS

Illustrations by Alison Kendall

Contact Andrew Martinez at drewart@gmail.com.

1. Begin with an empty stove.

Remove all the stove parts and clean the cabinet inside and out.

2. Make the shelves.

Measure the stove's interior depth and width. Use a saw to cut masonite shelves to size. Attach 2 corner brackets to each shelf using nuts and bolts, with washers if desired. Hold each shelf to the interior of the stove to determine placement. Mark spots for the bracket holes with a crayon or pencil (be sure shelves are level). Drill holes in the stove at each spot that you marked, and attach the shelves with nuts and bolts.

3. Mount it to the wall.

Drill 4 holes in the back of the stove and 4 matching holes on the wall. If your stove has bulges on the bottom that act as feet, these are great spots for screws to attach to the wall. Insert drywall anchors into the wall, then screw through the stove and into the anchors to securely mount the cabinet.

4. Optional towel holder.

Using the existing hole previously occupied by the stove's gas valve, slide a loop of vinyl-coated "aircraft cable" through to act as a towel holder. A standard U-bolt cable clamp can be used to secure it on the inside. ✗

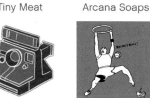

Etsy

Glass
GreenLanternGlass $65

Bags & Purses
moop $78

Housewares
JoshuaStone $190

Paper Goods
heatherjeany $12

Accessories
cipolla $45

Jewelry
pirilamporiscado $78

Ceramics & Pottery
melabo $45

Bath & Body
tworiverssoaps $5

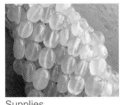

Supplies
ollieandjo $12

Geekery
lupin $8

Bags & Purses
feeldesign $95

Jewelry
simonewalsh $52

Children
jujuw $13

Plants & Edibles
cravelouisiana $10

Ceramics & Pottery
trixiedelicious $25

Jewelry
gemmafactrix $10

Art
keelyart $625

Supplies
mamacitabeadworks $4

Lighting
LightingArtGallery $390

Bags & Purses
LadybugSF $36

Accessories
lotusjewelrystudio $95

Jewelry
zulasurfing $600

Art
Artsy $88

Jewelry
brookemarton $26

Etsy.com
Your place to buy and
sell all things handmade™

Knitting
saralagace $36

Accessories
zerkahloostrah $425

Furniture
bellaglass $2,900

Art
elsita $20

Music
ArmorGuitars $1,500

Paper Goods
jengsshop $8.50

Ceramics & Pottery
MaggieWeldonInc $56

Accessories
katieburley $95

Accessories
loobyloucrafts $39

Supplies
loop $15

Jewelry
esdesigns $15

Clothing
danishknitdesign $144

Children
plainlyjane $56

Ceramics & Pottery
kimwestad $150

Accessories
workingclassheroes $29

Housewares
Lalitah $32

Buy Handmade

These items are some of the over **900,000 handmade goods and supplies** for sale on Etsy.
Find any of the items above for sale, each in their own shop. Go to: shopname.etsy.com

Bathroom Made Cozier

When **Sarah Knouse** moved into her "dreary, cookie-cutter" apartment, the 24-year-old art school graduate was determined to spruce it up, "particularly my bleak and shabby bathroom." As a collector of old crafting magazines, Knouse was inspired by the "strange extended family of cozies" that were big in the 70s, and decided to cozy up her bathroom.

"The cozy is made of plastic netting that has been soldered together to fit the contours of my bathroom and all of its fixtures," Knouse explains. "Colorful yarn has been woven through the netting to create an ultra-large cozy, similar to the tissue-box cozies I grew up with in my home. And like a traditional tissue-box cozy, the bathroom cozy can be removed from the space for which it was designed, and displayed in a separate location while still keeping its form."

Thankfully, Knouse wasn't alone in her mission. At her "cozy parties," which offered free food including 40 pounds of ice cream "to those who proved worthy," many friends — and strangers — helped Knouse stitch yarn through thousands of tiny plastic squares, which "became a painfully slow and tedious marathon."

Although she now considers her project "an amazing feat of craft," she says she doesn't recommend the project to anyone, ever. "It was, for the most part, an excruciatingly miserable and almost masochistic experience that, looking back, I can laugh at."

—Carla Sinclair

Photograph by Sarah Knouse